BFI Film Classics

The BFI Film Classics series introduces, interprets and celebrates landmarks of world cinema. Each volume offers an argument for the film's 'classic' status, together with discussion of its production and reception history, its place within a genre or national cinema, an account of its technical and aesthetic importance, and in many cases, the author's personal response to the film.

For a full list of titles in the series, please visit
https://www.bloomsbury.com/uk/series/bfi-film-classics/

For Guy, Yena, Dominic and Benjamin

# Die Hard

Jon Lewis

THE BRITISH FILM INSTITUTE
Bloomsbury Publishing Plc, 50 Bedford Square, London, WC1B 3DP, UK
Bloomsbury Publishing Inc, 1385 Broadway, New York, NY 10018, USA
Bloomsbury Publishing Ireland, 29 Earlsfort Terrace, Dublin 2, D02 AY28, Ireland

BLOOMSBURY is a trademark of Bloomsbury Publishing Plc

First published in Great Britain 2025 by Bloomsbury on behalf of the
British Film Institute, 21 Stephen Street, London, W1T 1LN
www.bfi.org.uk

The BFI is a cultural charity, a National Lottery distributor, and the UK's lead organisation for film
and the moving image. We believe society needs stories. Film, television and the moving image
bring them to life, helping us to connect and understand each other better. We share the stories
of yesterday, search for the stories of today, and shape the stories of tomorrow.

A catalogue record for this book is available from the British Library.

A catalog record for this book is available from the Library of Congress.

ISBN:   PB:   978-1-8390-2652-2
        ePDF:  978-1-8390-2654-6
        ePUB:  978-1-8390-2653-9

Printed and bound in India

For product safety related questions contact productsafety@bloomsbury.com.

To find out more about our authors and books visit www.bloomsbury.com
and sign up for our newsletters.

# Contents

# Introduction

The original trailer for *Die Hard* promised a political thriller torn from the headlines: 'Within this skyscraper high above the city, twelve terrorists have declared war.' We discover thirty minutes into the film that the mooted terrorist siege is merely a deception. *Die Hard* is in fact *just* a caper film, but that fact is in the final analysis less important than it should be.

Towards the end of the film, Holly (Bonnie Bedelia) discovers the truth about her captors. She remarks to Hans (Alan Rickman), the gang's ruthless leader, with disappointment: 'You're nothing but a common thief.' He takes offence and replies: 'I am an exceptional thief.' He's right about that. But what he doesn't bother to tell her is that once upon a time not so long ago he was in fact a terrorist. His career change is another of the film's several anticlimaxes – apropos a terrorist thriller that is just a caper film. That one might begin one's career as a terrorist and end it as a thief was in 1988 a matter of wishful thinking. Greed and self-interest were easier for American filmgoers to understand than politics. And to be fair, while the crime at hand in *Die Hard* is not ostensibly political, Hans's attitude towards his adversaries still is.

In its misdirection – a caper film promoted as a political thriller – *Die Hard* nonetheless expressed widely shared anxieties in the US concerning international security and stability, anxieties rooted in a seeming decline in American prestige and influence that would eventually fall under the rubric 'the war on terror'. There were before its release already iterations of that war, the hostage crisis at the American Embassy in Tehran, which lasted from 4 November 1979 to 11 January 1981, only the most worrying example. Reports on the evening news of terrorist cells operating undercover in European cities like Frankfurt and Rome were disconcerting as well.

These stories more directly fuelled the terrorist subtext in *Die Hard*. When, early in the film, a TV newscaster offers some backstory on Hans, she traces his biography to a German terrorist organisation called the Volksfrei Movement. She runs with the terrorist story, along with most everyone else in the film, because what's happening at the Nakatomi Plaza looks a lot like a terrorist attack: hostage-taking, hostage-killing; negotiations with and demands made to law enforcement and federal authorities seeking the release of political prisoners; men speaking a language other than English laying siege to a commercial site, wielding automatic weapons, assembling and employing rocket launchers to shoot things out of the sky.

The group's name, Volksfrei, roughly translates as 'People's Freedom', but the name's not important as the organisation did not exist. Volksfrei was meant to stand in for a very real German terrorist outfit formed amidst the student protest movement in Germany in the late 1960s: the Red Army Faction (Rote Armee Fraktion), which became better known worldwide as the Baader–Meinhof Group. Named after two of its founders, Andreas Baader and Ulrike Meinhof, who became the group's enduring martyr after she was found dead in her jail cell in 1976, the group first made headlines in 1967 protesting the Shah of Iran's visit to Berlin. The activists regarded the Iranian strongman as an American puppet (a view later shared by the Tehran Embassy hostage-takers as well) and symbol of the United States' military and political sphere of influence. The events of the subsequent German Autumn – a series of robberies, bombings and murders perpetrated by the Baader–Meinhof Group deemed a national crisis in 1977 – were rooted in an anti-Americanism as well. The centrepiece of the German Autumn was the abduction and murder of the industrialist Hanns Martin Schleyer, a former Nazi SS officer installed with American support as the head of the Confederation of German Employers' Associations. The kidnap and murder of Schleyer was meant to express a frustration at American meddling in West Germany's domestic affairs, especially the reintegration back into the political and economic mainstream of Schleyer and other anti-Communist former Nazis.

The ideology behind the Baader–Meinhof Group was anti-fascist, anti-police, anti-NATO and anti-American – as were, or so it seemed to many Americans in the 1980s, most every terrorist group at the time. European terrorism characterised by the Baader–Meinhof gang and Italy's Brigate Rosse, which made front-page news in the US after the 1978 kidnapping and murder of the former prime minister Aldo Moro, emerged out of Cold War political and military instabilities and fears of American ideological hegemony.

Andrew Britton's brilliant essay, 'Blissing Out: The Politics of Reaganite Entertainment',[1] written two years before the release of *Die Hard*, provides a blueprint for the reactionary American cinema that coalesced in response to this global ideological instability and in concert with the Reagan–Bush regime's promise to restore America's standing in the new world order, exploiting the advent of glasnost reforms in the Soviet Union, the fall of the Berlin Wall and, counterintuitively, in anticipation of an emerging hot war on terror, with the permanent warfare state aimed at a new cast of antagonists. *Die Hard* narrativises redress for perceived postwar slights, for a decline in American international prestige, economic super-power status and, after Vietnam, military eminence. The fate of things in *Die Hard* comes down to a lone-wolf hero, a most American of American heroes: 1980s man of action, John McClane (Bruce Willis). He is working class, libertarian/objectivist, anti-authoritarian, anti-intellectual, impulsive and improvisational. Like Indiana Jones, another icon of Britton's Reaganite cinema, he's a throwback to a time when men were (allowed to be) men. Times had been rough for John in the lead-up to the events that unfold in *Die Hard*, much as they had been for the US as well. But when the chips are down, the film assures us, John (this quintessentially American hero) is the sort of guy we (the world, that is) will surely want and need. *Die Hard* is Britton's Reaganite 'bliss out' par excellence.

The real politics of real European-based terrorists were for most Americans too complex and too integrally tied to arcane *foreign* politics to effectively integrate into the *Die Hard* story. So, the film-makers instead smartly highlighted a single, and deeply worrying, sidebar: the connections between German terrorists (like the Baader–Meinhof Group, like the fictional Volksfrei) and the Palestine Liberation Organisation (PLO) – a terrorist group that in 1988 most Americans (given the ample news coverage on Israel) knew plenty about. As early as 1970 there were photographs in newspapers of Baader–Meinhof gang members training at a PLO boot camp in Jordan. The PLO gave the Baader–Meinhof Group international street cred. And *Die Hard* exploited that.

The confluence of European-based political radicals, the PLO, and other Middle Eastern and North African terrorists would be front-page news everywhere in the world some six months *after* the release of *Die Hard*, just in time for Christmas (the ostensible setting for the film), when the news broke that Pan Am Flight 103 had exploded over Lockerbie, Scotland. As the story unravelled, *Die Hard*'s seeming premise, its initial promise of a terrorist action traced to ruthless, well-armed German-based terrorists trained or backed or in conspiracy with jihadists in the Middle East and North Africa, seemed with the Lockerbie news eerily prescient.

A quick recap: on 21 December 1988, shortly after Flight 103's scheduled 7 pm departure from London's Heathrow Airport, a bomb planted on the plane by German-based, Libyan-financed terrorists in Frankfurt detonated. The blast killed all 243 passengers and 16 crew members, as well as 11 residents of the Scottish town. The terrorist premise of *Die Hard* is never fulfilled on screen. Over Lockerbie, it was ... and with geographic and geopolitical similarities to the film that were difficult to miss. In *Die Hard*, the former terrorists have no politics. Rooted as well in Frankfurt, the real terrorists most certainly did.

When, in *Die Hard*, Hans boasts that he has the same tailor as the PLO leader Yasser Arafat, the remark is meant to imply Hans's personal acquaintance with the notorious figure. That they are fellow terrorists under their fine wool apparel is another bit of misdirection, as the line seems meant to reveal the hypocrisy of all so-called freedom fighters – like Arafat and his fictional ally Hans – men of the people who share a fondness for expensive bespoke suits from Savile Row. Hans is, this time at least, in it for the money, not the glory or the political capital. Nonetheless, dropping Arafat's name into a 1988 movie was even before Lockerbie no small gesture. After 21 December 1988, it seemed positively clairvoyant. *Die Hard*, as Britton cautioned about Reaganite cinema in general, was never 'just entertainment'.

I first saw *Die Hard* late in its first run, after Lockerbie, after a simple twist of fate on 21 December 1988 proved for me, too, a matter of life or death. In early December 1988 I completed a semester teaching in an international programme at what was back then Bath College of Higher Education (now Bath Spa University). My wife Martha and I decided to squeeze in a couple of weeks of travel around Europe before heading back to London to catch a flight to the US. We narrowed our itinerary down to two flights with two different destinations: Pan Am Flight 123, a direct flight over the pole from Heathrow to Seattle, Washington, connecting after that to a commuter flight to Portland, Oregon, near where we live, set to depart in the morning on 22 December; and Pan Am 103, scheduled to depart the previous evening, stopping in New York before continuing on to Detroit, where Martha's parents lived and with whom we'd then spend Christmas. After six months working and living abroad, we decided to go straight home. So, we booked Flight 123. Every time I screen *Die Hard*, and now here again as I write this monograph for the BFI, I remember waking up in a friend's flat in Stoke Newington on 22 December 1988 to the news on the radio. But for the grace of … we could have been on that plane.

# 1 Police and Thieves

*Die Hard* begins with the story of a marriage on the rocks. The arrival of the gang takes us away from that marriage, as personal matters pale with the arrival of something bigger, louder and more interesting to watch. The implied promise, of course, is that the stakes and conflicts evinced in the A- and B-plots (the crime story and the marriage story, respectively) will eventually intersect or overlap and then both be solved in the film's climax. Someone has driven a van into John and Holly's marriage and only after dealing with what the van has brought into their lives can they, whom we meet separately and then together in the film's extended opening, sort out their fraught relationship. Much as we recognise the formula, we welcome the fundamental promise that both conflicts will be resolved not in wordy arbitration, but in action instead. *Die Hard* is an American film. With violence being the most effective solution to everyone's problems.

Action films as well as political thrillers – the genres in play in the A-story – work best when they seem realistic. Here again, *Die Hard* proved not only realistic but prescient. Parking garages in otherwise secure office buildings, we would all discover a few years later, were in fact vulnerable to intruders, to terrorists. For the first World Trade Center bombing in 1993, a device was rigged to a van (that had arrived much as Hans and his gang arrive in *Die Hard*). The real-world terrorists then abandoned their vehicle and exited the site unnoticed (at least initially). The bomb they planted in the van later detonated, the impact targeting the North Tower. The charge was meant to be powerful enough to topple one twin tower into the other. While that didn't happen, the blast nonetheless killed six people and over 1,000 others were injured. *Die Hard* elaborates a similar arrival at a similar target – a skyscraper leased to businesses engaged in, and to a larger extent representing, American-headquartered global capital. The film revealed how easily one might enter such a building without engaging security ... much as the real terrorists in New York City would five years later.

John McTiernan's action editing – the ever-quickening pace of shots from multiple camera angles edited into a spatial and temporal continuity – highlights the gang's arrival. Like the characters he introduces, McTiernan, too, is expert at staging action. We cut from the van's arrival to the ground-floor lobby as Karl and Theo, a white European terrorist/mercenary (we think he's the former, but he's actually the latter – another misdirection) and a Black American tech genius, make their entrances. Theo prattles loudly about the Los Angeles Lakers basketball game the night before. The discourse distracts the lone concierge/security officer behind the front desk. Once in range, Karl pulls out a gun and without a moment's hesitation kills the concierge in cold blood. He and his cohorts mean business ... but what sort of business will not be clear for a while.

Akin to other caper films like *The Asphalt Jungle* (John Huston, 1950) or *Oceans 11* (Lewis Milestone, 1960, and Steven Soderbergh's superior remake, 2001), these men are experts at specific, peculiar tasks. Karl makes easy work of the killing. Theo takes a seat behind the console and quickly seizes control of the technology in the building. We then cut to Hans (and actor Alan Rickman) making the most of his entrance. Like so many arch criminals in American films, one of his crimes will be chewing the scenery. He enters the Nakatomi Tower only after the messy violence is complete, but that too is a misdirection, as we discover that, unlike many of the masterminds we've met at the movies, the act of killing comes easily to him.

The next gang member we meet is Tony, whose job is to disconnect the phone system – back then, analogue. There are dozens of wires to sort through and he takes his time to be careful and precise. He talks to himself in German – a first hint at the specific ethnicity of the gang. Fair to wonder: how do master criminals like Hans assemble their gangs? Where did he find Karl? Tony? Theo? What's in it for the henchmen? With terrorists, we assume they are

all true believers. But Hans's gang are not terrorists, at least not anymore. Is it the money, then? Are there mercenaries for hire out there no matter the megalomaniacal, crackpot scheme? We who do not live in an action film will never know.

Tony sorts the colour-coded wires. Karl gets impatient and uses a chainsaw to cut them all in a single swipe. We've seen enough already to know that Karl is the gang member we need to keep an eye on. Karl will later have it out with John, twice. These two men – the hero and the villain's soldier, his heavy – are in some basic ways alike. Neither takes orders well. Neither knows when to quit. Karl is played by the charismatic ballet dancer and Soviet defector Alexander Godunov. He's beautiful. He's famous. And like the film, he and his defection are pulled from recent headlines.

We cut to John washing up in an executive bathroom and for the first but not last time find him eyeing his reflection in the mirror. These are men – he and Karl – who like what they see when they look in the mirror. Glass mirrors, windows and partitions, intact and then broken, will be important throughout. That's being set up here as well.

We cut to Hans in the lobby, then back to John. The logic of the cutting and the costuming makes clear their differences: a man in a perfectly tailored suit and another barefoot in a wife-beater T-shirt – a look sported as well by Stanley Kowalski and Sonny Corleone.[2]

Marlon Brando in his wife-beater T-shirt in *A Streetcar Named Desire* (1951)

The costuming of Willis and Rickman surely marks their difference. John hasn't seen the van pull into the garage or Karl and Theo take over the lobby. His attention is currently focused on Holly. When he calls the limo driver, Argyle, the first of two Black buddies in the film, he knows his fate in the short term is not in his hands. But he doesn't know the half of it. He tells Argyle to wait until he has a clearer picture of where he will need to go after the party. The phone call cuts out the moment Karl saws through the phone lines.

Argyle thinks John has hung up on him. And he doesn't give it a
second thought. He's on the clock, after all. If this is a statement on
race, on young Black men in America, it's not altogether flattering:
Argyle is feckless, happy to party on in the limo and pick up his
hourly pay cheque. But that's not what McTiernan is up to here.
We need to be patient with the race card. And with Argyle. As once
Argyle understands what's happened, he will quite literally crash his
way into the action. But that's still over ninety minutes away.

    We cut to an elevator as it heads up to the Nakatomi Christmas
party on the 30th floor. The gang cock their automatic weapons. We
hear the click-click sound endemic to the action genre of guns made
ready. A slow zoom-in on Hans prompts a cut to a medium close-up
of John, wondering at the lost connection to Argyle. We stay with
John, so it is with him that we first hear the sounds of automatic
weapon fire and of a woman screaming. John, still shoeless and
undressed to his T-shirt, grabs his pistol.

    We cut to the gang rounding up the party guests. The gang speak
among themselves in German. The dialogue is not subtitled because
we are meant to experience what's happening along with the hostages
and John, who, like most American filmgoers, don't understand what
they are saying. We see Holly in close-up, highlighted among the

Holly in close-up – alone in a crowd

rioting partiers, worried but calm. McTiernan will photograph Holly/ Bedelia this way a lot in the film, in close-ups and medium close- ups, alone in a crowd, worried but calm, including in the climactic confrontation between Hans and John. Holly is capable on the job and off, in the family melodrama and in the action film. She's surely the right woman for John. But is he the right man for her?

John heads up the stairs to the 32nd floor. Early in the film, the security guard provides John with details about the structure of the Nakatomi Tower. This bit of expository dialogue is not innocuous, as McTiernan never wastes our time. When the shit hits the proverbial fan, we know only as much about the Nakatomi Tower as John gleans from this brief conversation in the lobby. His instinct seems initially to match ours, to get away from the danger. But it is also different, as he heads up and above the fray instead of down and out of the building to safety.

Once he has ascended to temporary safety, John pauses to talk to himself. The riffing – the clever asides aloud and to himself – pervade the film. These neatly alluded to and organically grew out from Willis's

*Moonlighting* (1985–9)

character, the private detective David Addison, on the popular ABC-TV series *Moonlighting*. The show, which ran for sixty-seven episodes from March 1985 to May 1989, frequently broke the fourth wall, with the actors, Willis and his co-star Cybill Shepherd, in and sometimes out of character, speaking directly to the TV audience, acknowledging an awareness of performing roles in the fictional world of the TV story and in the production of a show for a major American television network. *Moonlighting* successfully built upon the unlikely sexual tension between the former model turned businesswoman Maddie Hayes (Shepherd) and Willis's wise-cracking macho detective, an odd-couple relationship that surely foregrounded Holly and John, the successful businesswoman and her wise-cracking detective husband.

The opening sequence runs for over eight minutes, punctuated finally as we cut back to the Christmas party. The revellers are now hostages. Hans is in control. He reads from a prepared statement that is not as helpful as the hostages or we at the time think it is. As it is another misdirection. The speech is boilerplate movie-terrorist prattle: a pat anti-capitalist screed. Are Hans's or the screenwriter's ideas really this half-baked? We wonder. Hans tells the hostages that he has come to the Nakatomi Plaza to teach them and their corporate employers a lesson about 'the real use of power'. Terrorist or thief, he is telling the truth about that.

This latest misdirection builds upon assumptions the hostages, John and the American film audience have about terrorists *and* about foreigners in general. Hans is banking on the other characters in the film making the same assumptions. His plan is not about politics. It's about property: bonds, buildings, hardware. That's why as characters sequentially discover the truth, they are disappointed even as the basic conditions of the narrative don't change all that much. Terrorists or thieves, the gang plan to kill everyone who gets in their way.

The primary plotline effectively conflates political terrorism with capital manipulation, two different crimes endemic to the 1980s. Hans is plotting to steal the ridiculous sum of $640 million, which refigures this terrorist villain as an embodiment of Reagan-era greed. Once upon a time, Hans believed in something. Now he just believes in money. The deregulated economics accompanying 'the Reagan revolution' enabled the acquisition of vast fortunes by unscrupulous financiers, white-collared thieves like Hans, while everyday working people, like John in his sleeveless T-shirt, toiled in relative poverty and irrelevance. John's problem with authority is something he shares with plenty of other 1980s heroes, most aptly here the similarly libertarian Snake Plissken in John Carpenter's *Escape from New York* (1981), who saves the planet while never '[giving] a fuck' about politics. In fighting Hans, John performs an explicitly anti-finance-class rebellion, a struggle against a system corrupted by money. But even that Me-Decade critique carries with it a timely Reaganite anti-big-government message. Flipping back to the Reagan script, John's fight against financial thieves requires a parallel struggle against inept government agents. John is in the end a lone hero fighting everyone over everything.

Hans singles out Takagi, the top-ranking Nakatomi executive on site, and takes him away from the group. He plans to coerce information that will help him open the company's safe.

First, a little backstory on the executive is introduced into the film. And it's not incidental. Here again, McTiernan doesn't waste our time. Takagi, along with his parents, we are told, were among those

Japanese Americans interned during the war. Hans is, we still believe, an anti-American terrorist, so we assume he sees Takagi as a fellow victim of American imperial power. Takagi corrects that assumption; he sees himself as a successful global businessman living in the present, looking towards the future. He is nobody's victim. Like so many Japanese men after the war, he has made his peace with imperial America and made the most of the postwar economic recovery. That the skyscraper under siege has taken its name from the Japanese company he helps run highlights his and his countrymen's success.

The sleek branding characteristic of Japanese companies operating in the US in the 1980s is epitomised by the superb Nakatomi Plaza logo, which is widely celebrated in graphic design circles.[3] The logo depicts a samurai helmet that dovetails neatly with the design of the building (the real Fox Plaza building in LA and the fictitious Nakatomi Tower). Apropos modern Japanese capitalist enterprise, and in comparison to the American corporations lagging behind, the logo/branding is everywhere: an exterior plaque, on the walls and floors, on the table John hides under and shoots through to vanquish an adversary.

Takagi leads a mostly American supporting staff; tables turned, but – and this is surely a subtext to the film – not for long.

The logo displayed on the directory screen

In short order, Takagi will be dead. Holly, a modern American woman, will take charge of operations in his stead. The building that sports the Nakatomi logo will soon be in dire shape thanks to explosions on the roof and near its base. John, the film's all-American hero, has supervised much of the carnage and toddles off into a new dawn disinterested in the clean-up he's helped make necessary. Wishful nativist thinking, really ... but *Die Hard* is at bottom an all-American fantasy.

McTiernan wants us to track the ethnic backstories, as this is a movie about them versus us. When Hans leads Takagi away from the rest of the hostages, he hums the fourth movement of Beethoven's Symphony No. 9, the 'Ode to Joy'. He's ever so German. Hans peers longingly at the safe; a first hint that he's a thief not a freedom fighter. That fact will become clear to us shortly. But first, some small talk. Hans comments on Takagi's suit: 'John Phillips, London ... rumor has it, Arafat buys his there.' We cut to John, still shoeless and shirtless, still ascending the building's exoskeleton. The cut visually contextualises the comment; it is yet another comparison between the adversaries – a comparison Hans will persist in making, disparaging John and the Reagan-era-cowboy iteration of America John so epitomises, so represents. The cut also establishes geographic continuity: where John is and where he is going as Hans and Takagi have their moment.

John ascends to the 35th floor and stumbles upon a few gang members and then spies what they have brought with them: guided missiles! We see things from John's point of view here, and the evidence has him, and us, thinking still that these men must be terrorists. In a few minutes we will know more than he does – and, indeed, we will know more than John until the climax of the film – but we nonetheless tend to read scenes with John in mind: the scenes he is in and the scenes that transpire out of his view and out of his ability to control, the scenes he improvises better than we would, as well as those he misreads because we know things he doesn't.

Hans's exchange with Takagi offers a little backstory on Hans as well. We won't get, and maybe don't need, much more. The two men enter an office and Hans admires an architect's model laid out on a table. 'I used to make models as a boy,' Hans muses. Of course he did. Hans expresses affection for 'exactness ... the attention to every detail'. Takagi thinks Hans is an anti-capitalist terrorist, so he tries to justify the project displayed on the table as something other than economic exploitation. Hans tells Takagi that he believes him, that he read about the project in *Forbes*, hardly the sort of magazine we'd expect a German anti-capitalist terrorist to read.

Then Hans gets down to business: 'I could talk about industrialization and men's fashions all day, but I'm afraid work must intrude.' Hans wants the access code to the safe. Takagi thinks Hans is plotting a cybercrime – something very new in 1988 – and that he plans to use the purloined information for terrorist blackmail. When Hans continues, 'I need the code because I am interested in the $640 million in negotiable bearer bonds that you have in your vault,' it hits Takagi sideways. 'You want money?' he asks. 'What kind of terrorists are you?' Rickman milks the payoff line: 'Who said we were terrorists?' McTiernan has timed this revelation perfectly: we are thirty minutes in.

The ostensible objects of interest in the vault are bearer bonds, fixed-income securities few filmgoers then as now have ever seen or know anything about. A quick sidebar, then: bearer bonds were introduced after the American Civil War and what makes them unique is that they are not registered to an owner; they belong to whomever has the physical certificate in their possession. Like cash.

In the little time we have to think about such things as filmgoers, Hans's plot to take possession of the bearer bond certificates *seems* to make sense. Once they are in his possession, they are indeed *his*. Moreover, the plot to steal such an obscure financial instrument – something rare and valuable – elevates the crime dramatically in the script and in the fictional world of the film. But to nitpick, in the US in 1988, stealing bearer bonds really didn't make much sense. Bearer bonds were discontinued by the US government in 1982 under the Tax Equity and Fiscal Responsibility Act, mostly due to their frequent misuse for money laundering and tax evasion. In 1988, holders of government bearer bonds could redeem them only through the US Treasury. Corporate bearer bonds were even more difficult to negotiate as a certificate holder would have to work directly with the company that issued them.[4] For obvious reasons, Hans would not be able to work directly with the US Treasury to secure redemption of stolen property. And if the bonds were corporate and issued by Nakatomi, it is hard to imagine why the company would negotiate redemption with him either.

Takagi refuses to give Hans the code. He says he doesn't know it, and that may well be true. It doesn't matter. 'You'll just have to kill me,' Takagi tells Hans, and, ever practical, Hans complies. McTiernan cuts away from the kill-shot, but not as a matter of sensibility. He does so to show us John, who witnesses the murder. We see John, whom Hans can't see, react in a tight close-up. And it is instructive. Even a hard-nosed cop like him is astonished, repulsed. No shame, then, that we are too.

Soon after witnessing Hans's murder of Takagi, John contacts Hans on the two-way radio. John's aggressive banter takes Hans by surprise; us too. 'Who are you?' Hans asks, and then answers his own question: 'Just another American who's seen too many movies as a child. Another orphan of a bankrupt culture who thinks he's John Wayne. Rambo. Marshall Dillon.' (He is right about John and plenty of other American men too.) John plays along. Ignoring the old world/new world paradigm, the anti-Americanism consistent with Hans's past and current masquerade as a terrorist, John focuses on a random detail and says he prefers the more old-school Roy Rogers. 'Do you really think you have a chance against us, cowboy?' Hans asks. This is something they teach in Screenwriting 101, as it is a question the audience is asking too. John replies by going non-linear – taking us from the intro class to a more advanced seminar: 'Yippee-ki-yay motherfucker.' Hans speaks English fluently. But the idiom is beyond the pale, and for the moment it stops the conversation dead.

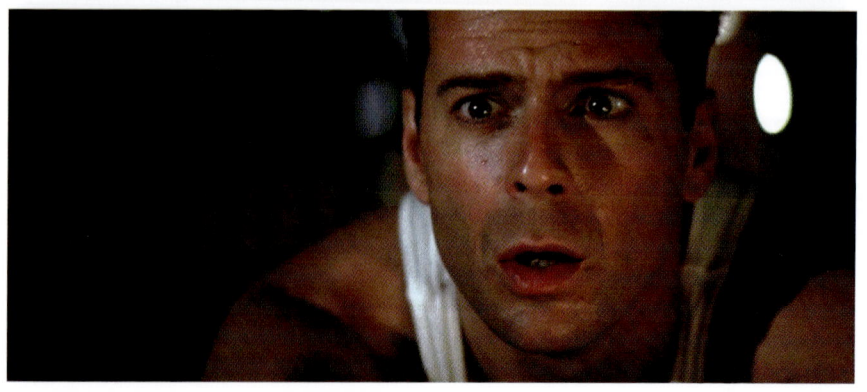

Hans's dismissive attitude about American pop culture cuts two ways. In a rambling monologue to Takagi, he recalls Alexander the Great weeping as he realises there are no more worlds to conquer. He muses on 'the benefits of a classical education'. John, on the other hand, is very much as Hans describes him, the product of too many hours watching American movies and TV. Education classical or otherwise won't be a deciding factor here. In Reagan's America, intellect is in tandem with arrogance, with overconfidence, with elitist airs, with a lack of common sense. Hans knows a fine suit when he sees one and can allude to Alexander's conquest of the ancient world. But he confuses iconic Hollywood storylines and misidentifies celebrities. Pop culture is beneath him. *Die Hard* pits old-world arrogance against new-world pluck, book smarts against street smarts. It's 1988. And anti-elitism is already an action genre convention. And Hans is in an action film.

Later, when a local television news crew picks up the unfolding story of a 'terrorist takeover of the Nakatomi building', the on-air reporter updates Hans's CV: 'Sources say that the terrorist leader may be this man, Hans Gruber, a member of the radical Volksfrei Movement …'; then: 'Strangely, the Volksfrei leadership issued a communiqué an hour ago stating that Gruber had been expelled from that organization.' Because the latter phrase doesn't fit the narrative, it is left dangling. McTiernan then cuts to the Black Los Angeles policeman Al talking to John on the two-way. This is the second time we've been told that Hans is not what he seems, that he is not a terrorist. And the second time McTiernan has staged scenes to make clear that John is not privy to this information.

Hans kills Takagi after telling him he's not a terrorist. Elsewhere, because it suits the caper, he persists with the fiction that he and his gang are terrorists. At 1 hour and 20 minutes in to the film, he issues demands to Deputy Dwayne Robinson, a bumbling LAPD hostage negotiator: the release of political prisoners held in US jails, along with a list of men and women from Northern Ireland, Quebec and Sri Lanka, ending with 'the nine members of the Asian

Dawn', a group so obscure that Karl, sitting alongside Hans, frowns quizzically as he quietly repeats the name aloud. Hans is only riffing here; what little he knows about the Asian Dawn, he later tells Karl, he's read in *Time* magazine.

Dwayne follows protocol, as if reading from a script. He's a bureaucrat, incapable of improvisation. He will need more time, he says. Hans, it turns out, is playing for time. He's playing Dwayne, too, as he plots a bait-and-switch. Hans's plan exploits the predictability of his adversaries. That's why he is more than a match for the LAPD and, later, the FBI. Hans is banking on the media following their script too. We see a news show hastily assembled to report on the developing story, complete with an expert author, a straw man introduced only to lampoon another product of a classical education. The expert prattles about 'hostage dependency' as McTiernan cuts to an image of the panicked Nakatomi staff. The cut neatly undermines the expert.

The FBI show up – 'regular', Hans quips, 'like clockwork'. He tells Theo not to worry. And we soon learn why. The FBI order the power to the building cut, per protocol. Hans has anticipated the move and fitted it into his plans. 'The circuits [to the impenetrable time-locked safe] that can't be cut', he calmly reports to Theo, 'are cut automatically in response to a terrorist incident.' Much as we recognise what sort of movie we are in, we should recognise as well what era it refracts: 1980s America and Reagan's anti-big-government brand of Republican Conservatism. With that in mind, like Hans we, too, expect the FBI to screw things up.

When John ascends to the roof, he discovers plastique and detonators set to blow the top off the building. He calls Al to relay his discovery that the bait-and-switch, what John calls a 'double cross', will not involve the gang's exit by helicopter off the roof. But his message doesn't get through and Al can't relay a message of his own to John – that the FBI have deployed the helicopters not to ferry hostages and terrorists per Hans's instructions, but to lay siege to the Nakatomi Tower. 'White Agent Johnson' – he too has a Black buddy, and comically, with the same last name as his – glibly predicts the siege will result in the death of 20–25 per cent of the hostages. It's not clear how he's arrived at the number. It seems just as likely that his manoeuvre will kill everyone.

How we feel about the arrival of helicopters depends on how confident we are in John's success and how suspicious we are of big government. The quick answer is 'very' on both counts. The feds' failure is prefigured for a couple of reasons: because it would be cinematically disappointing and because it undermines the cowboy hero. Agents of the federal government are, as Reagan cautioned, part of the problem, not the solution.

Reagan won his mandate in 1980 by exploiting President Jimmy Carter's failure to negotiate an end to the terrorist takeover of the American Embassy in Iran. Principal among his campaign promises, Reagan vowed to resolve the crisis and did so just as he took office in January 1981. After the terrorist action in Tehran, Reagan successfully associated negotiation with Carter, with failure, with weakness, with humiliation on the world stage, with an American masculinity damaged in Vietnam and corrupted and betrayed by inept big-government bureaucracy.

Dwayne initially endeavours to negotiate with Hans. He's a local cop and follows local protocol for hostage negotiation. The FBI take over and because they assume the gang are terrorists, following Reagan-era protocol, refuse to negotiate. Turns out, neither protocol – the cops negotiating or the FBI cutting power to the building – thwarts Hans. He instead exploits the rules of engagement and is vulnerable only to someone not bound by bureaucracy or protocols: the lone-wolf American hero, John.

We don't get much time to think about John's discovery of the rigged explosives or Al's attempt to alert him about the FBI's cockamamie plan, as Karl gets the drop on John. We have been anticipating this confrontation. And their mano-a-mano slugfest does not disappoint. The fight commences with a familiar affirmation: Karl intones, 'We are both professional … this is personal.' *Die Hard* is not

really or only about hostages and terrorists, cops and robbers, good and evil. It is about men sorting out a peculiar action-film notion of masculinity. And to settle such matters, we need a fight, a series of fights – pain, struggle, living with a death on your conscience.

The fight resembles in style and duration the climactic encounter in the pouring rain between Riggs and Mr Joshua in *Lethal Weapon* (Richard Donner, 1987), a film produced the previous year by Joel Silver and released by Fox, the producer and studio behind *Die Hard*. Both fights end the same way, with the villain only seemingly defeated, somehow surviving the hero's best shot only to be gunned down by an otherwise mild-mannered Black sidekick – the nearly retired Rog in *Lethal Weapon* and the temporarily gun-shy Al in *Die Hard*.

John and Karl's slugfest goes on for so long, McTiernan needs an insert: something to cut away to and then back from. In fact, he will need several. First, the FBI helicopter with Agents Johnson and Johnson. White Agent Johnson is elated and shouts into the intercom, 'Just like fucking Saigon.' The remark in 1988 is fraught, especially after the reality of Vietnam and its impact on American geopolitical confidence, and the war's devastating impact on the men who fought there – a matter taken up by Hollywood in the years leading up to *Die Hard* in *The Deer Hunter* (Michael Cimino, 1978), *Coming*

*Home* (Hal Ashby, 1978), the first two *Rambo* films (*First Blood* [Ted Kotcheff, 1982] and *Rambo: First Blood, Part II* [George P. Cosmatos, 1985]) and *Lethal Weapon*, in which Riggs's anomie and Joshua's criminal savagery are both rooted in whatever went on over there. We cut away and back again to show time passing, and to remind us that the struggle is monumental, outrageous. The fight plods on and we cut away again, this time to Holly, who is by this point Hans's hostage. She discovers here, at 1 hour and 50 minutes into the film, that Hans and his gang are not terrorists, that their motives are selfish, not political. 'You're nothing but a common thief,' she grouses to Hans. He takes offence, 'I am an exceptional thief, Mrs McClane.' In the mixed-up world of 1988 male crisis, such are the fragile egos, the desperate need to be respected for what one does, even if it's illegal, even as it serially disappoints.

A question lingers even after Holly discovers Hans's identity. She is in either scenario – terrorist or caper – a hostage. And her captivity awaits John's confrontation with Hans. As a proper Reagan-era hero, John will find himself in an impossible bind. He has things his way at the end only because he brings a gun to the negotiation. In doing so – in never intending to just talk – he is the man we need. The gun strapped behind his neck feels like an improvisation. But it's not. His plan is to rescue Holly and kill Hans. Or die trying.

## **2** Men in Love

In 1987, the development of a film based on the Roderick Thorp novel *Nothing Lasts Forever* (1979) fell to Lawrence Gordon, who after stepping down as Twentieth Century Fox president negotiated, as part of his exit, an independent production deal with the studio. Gordon began his career in B-pictures, working for Sam Arkoff at American International Pictures and later Arkoff International Pictures (both companies went by the same acronym, AIP), where he produced Martin Scorsese's *Boxcar Bertha* (1972) and John Milius's *Dillinger* (1973). Gordon quickly graduated from the B's and became a major studio player, producing the hugely successful 1982 action-comedy *48 Hours*, directed by his production partner Walter Hill for Paramount – a film with stylistic and thematic similarities to *Die Hard*, the film that emerged from his development of *Nothing Lasts Forever*.

Fox owned the option on *Nothing Lasts Forever* because it had nearly two decades earlier produced and distributed a film based on its prequel, a much better Thorp novel, *The Detective*. That film, adapted in 1968 by Abby Mann (a two-time Oscar winner for Stanley Kramer's *Judgment at Nuremberg*, 1961, and *Ship of Fools*, 1965, and later the showrunner for the popular TV cop show *Kojak*, 1973–8), was directed by Gordon Douglas and starred Frank Sinatra, who had appeared in Douglas's popular crime film *Tony Rome*, released the previous year.

*Nothing Lasts Forever* tells the story of Joe Leland, a retired police detective now working as a private security consultant, who travels from New York to Los Angeles to visit his daughter, who has invited him to her office Christmas party at the Klaxon Oil building, a posh corporate HQ situated in a downtown high-rise. While there, Joe stumbles upon a terrorist plot. In the novel's climactic scene,

Joe thwarts the terrorists but arrives too late to save his daughter, who tumbles off the roof of the building along with the terrorists' leader, Anton Gruber.

To get the project off the ground, Gordon hired a young screenwriter named Jeb Stuart. Among Stuart's many challenges was the invention of a B-story, something the novel didn't provide. *The Detective*, Stuart no doubt knew, was a much better and more complicated book. It gave Mann, a far more experienced screenwriter, plenty to work with. The crime that comprises the A-story in *The Detective* involves the clandestine gay male subculture – a controversial setting in the mid-1960s. Joe is thwarted on the job by incompetent, corrupt and homophobic fellow policemen and at home, in the B-story, by his wife Karen's ambition: her pursuit of higher education and, after that, working in a job that made use of that education. Joe succeeds in accommodating Karen's professional endeavours, but can't abide her promiscuity, depicted as nymphomania explicitly in the novel and only slightly more subtly in the film.

*Nothing Lasts Forever* begins with the Lelands already divorced. The relationship Joe flies cross-country to repair is not with Karen, but instead with their adult daughter. Despite a colourful history, Karen figures in *Nothing Lasts Forever* only in absentia, which seemed even at the outset of Stuart's adaptation a problem to be solved.

One afternoon, while pondering the Leland family dynamic, the script's missing B-story, Stuart got into an argument with his wife. After an exchange of harsh words, he stormed out and got on an LA freeway, where a chance encounter gave him a sign. As Stuart recounted to me in a 2013 interview,

I was thinking about how I'm going to apologize to my wife and suddenly I found myself stuck behind a flatbed truck with appliance boxes and I couldn't go right or left and then the truck hit something in the road and a refrigerator box came out of the back and landed in front of me in the freeway and I went through the box at sixty-five miles an hour. Fortunately, there was no refrigerator in the box. But as I pulled over to the side of the road, I realized that *Nothing Lasts Forever*, which became *Die Hard* [at that moment, really] ... [would be] about a thirty-two-year-old guy [like Stuart at the time] who didn't apologize to his wife when he should have and then something bad happens.[5]

The refrigerator box incident gave Stuart his B-story. He replaced the daughter in the script with the hero's estranged wife. To complicate that relationship, he ditched the nymphomania from *The Detective* and instead drew from something he had talked about with several of his divorced friends whose ex-wives had gone back to their birth (what were called back then, 'maiden') surnames. For these men and women, the name-change conveyed a message about an identity separate from their husbands' and implied, as Holly does in the film, a new professional identity as a working woman. A woman using her birth name seemed to Stuart a perfect way to characterise a faltering marriage, especially in a telegraphic medium like a script.

Early in the film, John McClane (the renamed Joe Leland) peers into the Nakatomi Tower's (for 1988) ultramodern computer-assisted directory and scrolls in search of his wife's name and office number. He discovers that Holly (a name better suited than Karen to the film's

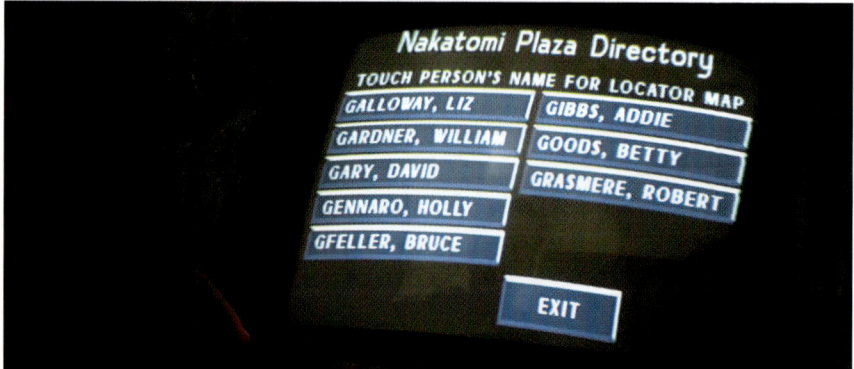

Christmas setting) has reverted to her birth surname, Gennaro, and feels deflated.

John's moment of shame, rejection and emasculation at the directory screen is complemented by a parallel scene elaborating Holly's preparation for his arrival. She is in her office, ducking away from the Christmas party to check in at home. She expects the housekeeper to pick up, but instead her daughter takes the call: 'McClane residence – Lucy McClane speaking.' Holly doesn't correct her. Holly later asks the housekeeper to make up the guest room. We gather this is not all John is hoping for. But Holly has her reasons. She's not sure what to expect. In fact, she's not even sure John will show up. We gather from Holly's conversation with the housekeeper that he hasn't bothered to call with his itinerary. 'Maybe he didn't have time,' she muses on the phone. But it's clear, he's been careless like this before.

John's arrival in LA exploits a familiar trope: he deboards a stranger in a strange land, a working-class, East Coast cop adrift in upmarket Century City – a theme *Beverly Hills Cop* (Martin Brest, 1984) nicely exploited for the action-film impresarios Don Simpson and Jerry Bruckheimer at Paramount four years earlier. In that film, a tough Detroit policeman, Axel Foley (Eddie Murphy), investigates the death of a childhood friend. A fish out of water in posh, politically correct Beverly Hills, Axel struggles against foreign mobsters *and* the protocols of the local police force. His brash manners and disdain for polite police procedure complicate matters in most every setting he wanders into. John feels similarly out of synch in sunny LA.

Argyle, the young Black temp limo driver, initiates an expository scene to set the film's B-story. There are things we need to know here at the start. Stuart and Steven E. de Souza, who was brought in to work from Stuart's draft, smartly opt for comedy to get the information out. Argyle: 'So, you divorced man?' John: 'Just drive the car.' Argyle (joking): 'She beat you up?' John: 'She had a good job. Turned into a great career.' The dialogue is not exactly linear and though the exchange is essentially good-natured, Argyle is taking pleasure in 'busting John's balls', as men are wont to do.

'So, you thought she wasn't gonna make it out here,' Argyle muses, then jokes that John is still waiting for her to come 'crawling back'. 'You're very fast, Argyle,' John says, though he knows better. John doesn't want to talk about Holly; he permits the misapprehension even as it makes him look bad, because it promises to end the conversation. The banter nonetheless establishes a friendship that will endure to the end of the film.

John's arrival is punctuated by what would become a familiar action-film ritual of introduction. In an executive washroom, John endeavours to wash off what the cross-country jet and limo rides and the scene at the concierge desk have done to his masculine composure. He strips to his T-shirt, and we get a first look at his (and of course the actor Bruce Willis's) particular brand of hard body. Mel Gibson in the previous year's *Lethal Weapon* begins his

Lean and hard-body Mel Gibson in a publicity photograph for *Lethal Weapon* (1987)

Arnold Schwarzenegger, the hardest of hard bodies, in *Terminator 2: Judgment Day* (1991)

quest with a similar display, meant at once for visual pleasure (for the mostly male audience, at that) and as an affirmation of his physical suitability for the task at hand.

Three years later, Arnold Schwarzenegger offered the apex of this trope in *Terminator 2: Judgment Day* (James Cameron), making the most of his entrance by dropping out of the sky fully (albeit rendered on camera, tastefully) nude – a hard body of extraordinary dimensions and in its prime. The Terminator's first order of business in the film is to find some clothes, which he acquires in a carefully shot fight with buff but lesser hard bodies (which in Schwarzenegger's case at the time included everyone else on earth). In *Die Hard*'s A-story John's hard body makes a narrative promise: he will have to be physically tough to survive. In the B-story, the value of his hard body will be more complicated.

McTiernan films the scene in variable focus, neatly blocking Holly and John. They were lovers not so long ago. So, John seems not to think twice about this brief, casual intimacy. But Holly does. Think twice, that is. We see Holly see John. And her reaction is instructive. It makes clear a sexual attraction and we surmise that this was never the problem for the two of them. (Something else was the problem. Still is.) The couple discuss politely where he will sleep during the visit. A matter of convenience and logistics. Both are careful not to reveal to the other how they feel. And that only highlights the tension, the intimacy. There's a palpable chemistry between the actors, Bedelia and Willis. The adept screenwriting and subtle acting make clear that the problem here is pride, not the mysteries of attraction.

Perhaps it is Willis's comic timing, which was so often on display in *Moonlighting*, that pushes the scene so surely into romantic comedy territory. Per the film theorist Brian Henderson's theory of the genre, these are characters who should be having sex but aren't. (Think: *It Happened One Night* [Frank Capra, 1934], *The Awful Truth* [Leo McCarey, 1937], *Bringing Up Baby* [Howard Hawks, 1938].) We watch romantic comedy, Henderson contends, anticipating the story's inevitable endpoint in which the characters come to realise what we have known from the start.[6] For a film filled with misdirections, we begin *Die Hard* with the promise of – as elaborated in another study of romantic comedy, Stanley Cavell's *Pursuits of Happiness* – a remarriage, a new start to an old relationship,[7] only to discover that's not really the film we're watching. Willis sells the comedy, though that won't be where he and we will be staying for long, as the narrative transitions first from comedy to a relationship melodrama (for a matter of just a few minutes) and then to the advertised action film. This unique ability to do or be in several films and genres at once would come to characterise Willis's considerable star persona, in evidence on the big screen from the release of *Die Hard* to his retirement in the 2020s.[8]

Regarding logistics, John tells Holly he's got a buddy in Pomona. He can stay there. That's nearly an hour's drive east – more, assuming Holly lives on the fashionable west side. It's a ridiculous plan and it suggests either that he has no intention of staying there or (just as likely, really) that he's flown cross-country without thinking much about what he'll do once he gets to LA. He certainly hasn't bothered to look at a map. This confidence in his ability to improvise will serve him well in the action film. Less so in the relationship melodrama or romantic comedy. We cut to a medium shot of Holly laughing at the prospect of John commuting from Pomona.

She invites him to stay in a 'spare bedroom'. We cut to a medium close-up of John in profile taking in the development. The continuity editing ensures that we read the offer as he does. Our rooting interests are firmly with him for the moment. We then cut back to Holly as she completes her thought; she is offering the guest bedroom because 'the kids would love to have [him] at the house'. This is a realistic reconciliation scene, and, not incidentally, good screenwriting here again. Both characters want to patch things up, but neither is willing to say so. Neither risk rejection. Neither risk seeming more eager than the other. We cut back to a medium close-up of John in profile. He takes the first risk, pressing what he sees as an advantage: 'They would, huh?' The tone implies he suspects the arrangement is not just for the kids.

Holly calls that bid and raises, adding sweetly: 'I would too.' They both recognise the romantic tension only to have the moment interrupted by two revellers stumbling in, hoping to find a private space for a hookup. The interruption derails the conversation and spoils the mood. There's a party going on around them, Holly's co-workers have reminded them of that. Holly and John need to get into the spirit of the season. So, they hatch a plan to get to her house in time to put the kids to bed. Family over business, a decision she and he haven't much favoured in the past. The plan implies what might and probably will happen after that. Again, she doubles down. 'I missed you,' she says, pointedly in the past tense, as after tonight she can be done with missing him.

Structure-wise, we know it's too early in the film for a reconciliation. Especially as John has flown cross-country to win an argument as well and as much as Holly's love. He knows how to be a man – just look at him – but not, we discover, a husband. In an imbalanced and oddly framed medium shot (note the abundance of negative space above and between them), the camera looks over Holly's shoulder (in the foreground), as we watch John kill the mood: 'I guess you didn't miss my name,' he says, 'except when you were signing [we gather, child support] checks.'

We cut to Holly's reaction in a variable focus medium shot, with John's blurry torso filling out the rest of the frame. She sighs. She's been *here* before. We feel deflated and see the relationship from her point of view. She begins explaining, for what we gather is not the first time, why she is calling herself Gennaro these days. It has nothing to do with him, she says. Nakatomi is a Japanese company and appearing independent will ease her ascent up the corporate ladder. The explanation gives John an out, a chance to circle back. But he doesn't take it. He needs to win the argument even if it keeps him out of her bed. We cut to a tighter shot of John, a close-up and in focus this time, as he stupidly presses the issue. The shot is framed to draw our attention to a detail that defines him as a cop and as a rugged action-film hero: a bullet-hole scar on his shoulder. Then back to the earlier shot of Holly in medium close-up and John out of focus – which is apt, as he has lost focus here. John has been invited to sleep over, with the implied promise that after tucking in their children, the distance between the guest room and Holly's bedroom might be easily bridged. Rekindling an old argument has made that eventuality remote. Holly remembers why she and John are separated, and says: 'Are we going to have this same conversation?' We are on her side now. Not his. We now know why she lives in LA. And why he doesn't.

Holly tries to make peace. She talks about 'what their marriage could be' if John wasn't so pig-headed, and we cut back to the medium shot of John over Holly's shoulder. It's an imbalanced composition, again highlighting negative space, referring to the distance that still exists between them. The scene is capped by the arrival of Holly's secretary, at once a reminder of her ascent in the company (she has a personal assistant) and a simple bit of stagecraft to end a scene that needs ending.

John is left alone, again – from his point of view, second fiddle to her career. He talks to himself aloud: 'That's great, John. Good job, very mature.' This bit of introspection reaffirms what we have only just witnessed: a domestic spat in which he's mostly, if not entirely, at fault. The self-deprecation makes clear that John is aware he has made matters worse. But not, apropos Stuart's refrigerator story, that he has any idea how to apologise.

In *The Detective*, Karen's serial infidelities make the marriage impossible. With the washroom scene and another early moment when Ellis hits on Holly and she rejects the advance as ridiculous, recognising (and how couldn't she?) that the fast-talking dealmaker is in no way *a man* like John, McTiernan makes clear that there is still only one guy for her. Holly still loves John. We see the sparks for

ourselves in the washroom scene. But first he will need to grow up and appreciate what he's already got.

Good thing, then, for John that the adventure story intervenes, and his introspection is necessarily abbreviated. The apology step or stage in their reconciliation is put off ... turns out, put off to the next two films in the franchise. McTiernan inserts ominous underscored music to cue the arrival of the van at the Nakatomi Plaza. With a simple filmic device, a sound cue, the director reveals how he wants us to read the larger sociodynamics of Holly and John's relationship, and by extension the many marriages in 1980s America complicated by working women in general. What the van brings to Nakatomi Plaza will remind Holly (and us) of John's value in and to a certain sort of storyline that will be (for him, for her, for everyone at the site), from this point on, a matter of life and death. Just how much John stands in for American men in general, just how much he represents American masculinity and a 1980s iteration of male panic or crisis, is a well-worn topic.[9] He enters the film as yet another cop on the edge, a variation on a theme set in motion in *Dirty Harry* (Don Siegel, 1971) and rebooted nearly two decades later in *Lethal Weapon* – a man of action beset by regulations and bureaucracies that complicate his performance on the job. His struggles, his ill-fittedness are depicted as a sad fact of neoliberal society, rooted in existential dread. The world has changed while he's been away – in John's case, while he was doing his bit on the mean streets of New York, not, as in so many other 1980s films, Indochina. While he was busy making his city safe, Holly has made a success of herself, moving along and ahead figuratively and geographically. Complicating matters are the apparent material rewards of her profession and the relative absence of same in his.

John is a rugged American hero. A veteran of the war on drugs, on terrorism, on crime. Like the Vietnam vet, like his predecessors Riggs and Dirty Harry Callahan, no one seems inclined to thank him for his service, even as that service has become, in a crime-ridden, terrorist-vulnerable America, ever more indispensable. Holly still finds John sexually interesting. But that's not enough anymore.

And he doesn't get why. She can't abide his meat-headedness, his arrogance, his pride, his immutability. Consequently, he begins the film wallowing in self-pity, self-annihilation and shame.

Shame is at once the least obvious and most telling aspect of John's, and by extension the 1980s American man's, predicament. Consider, as a mode of entry into that discussion, a particularly interesting 1998 interview for the *No Safe Place* documentary project at PBS with Robert Bly, the poet turned late twentieth-century oracle of masculinity. The *No Safe Place* project focused on violence against women, its myriad causes and some possible remedies. Bly, brought in to ponder strategies to combat the epidemic, opined that many men resort to violence as an incoherent response to feelings of shame. 'It takes a long time for men to learn to be able to talk about their shame,' Bly surmised. 'And sometimes … a woman will say a criticism to a man, perfectly ordinary criticism, and it goes into some shame place in the heart, and he can't get it back out.' His point here isn't that this shame is the woman's or more generally all women's fault, but rather that men have never learned to process their shame. And consequently, they revert to violence. Sometimes they direct it at women, apropos the context of the interview, or they direct it into violent professions or pursuits: in *Die Hard*, police work, the war on terror, the war on crime. As Bly concludes, 'It's easier to socialize a young man into being a warrior than a father.' John's predicament in a nutshell.

John has been trained at the police academy and before that, over years of socialisation in school, in sports, on the streets. So, he knows how to fight Hans and the gang. But how and where can he learn how to work things out with Holly? Bly poses this question with a ready answer: the media. And that leads to a different problem, as the media are bound to fail him. Hollywood films, including *Die Hard* it is worth noting, frequently depict men coping with their shame in the performance of violence. 'They are never going to learn responsible, gentle masculinity from the mass media or the television,' Bly concludes.[10]

Whenever a refrigerator box tumbles towards him – and this happens again and again in the film – John pauses to confront his shame: his failure with Holly, with the kids, with being a man. But then, when he discovers the box is empty, he escapes responsibility and puts off the consequences. He gets into and out of a series of scrapes, but much as it haunts his every move, he never figures out how to articulate or surmount this shame. That explains his behaviour in the executive washroom scene. He's stuck in a seeming biological imperative he can't see past, can't grow out of. He reacts. Instinctively. That's why he's so adept in the action scenes. And why he stumbles so when he's alone with Holly.

In John's reading of the cultural moment, Holly's dual identity, as she moves easily from Gennaro to McClane and back again, underlines his shame. That she goes by Gennaro on the job is a 'perfectly ordinary criticism' he can't abide, he can't pry loose from his broken heart. Bly's notion of *Iron John*, the title of his 1990 book and the source par excellence for various Men's Movements that built (albeit myopically or mistakenly) on it, was 'of a man who has been under water so long, he's become rusty'.[11] John to a T.

Clear throughout *Die Hard* is a cautionary fact: Holly is basically fine; John is not. This, too, fuels John's shame. The problem isn't the action at hand – the gang, the race against time, the idiot bureaucrats. It's the inevitable end to the current action and with it the free time to 'think, think, think' (as he says to himself when the action begins) that worry him so. Left alone with himself, with his thoughts, he descends all too easily into shame and an existential dread at what it means to be a man in Holly and the kids' lives, in a postmodern city like LA, in 1980s America. John is a dinosaur – he and men like him. And he has complex, irreconcilable feelings about that.

The action-film template allows for complex cultural and psychological issues to be resolved in the course of the programmatic plot. The action hero does the same things he's always done, maybe better this time. He says the same things he's said before – expressing his dominance in catchy two- or three-word quips. And yet here we are in 1988, in *Die Hard*: John is following the script, but nobody wants to give a hard-body hero a break, even and especially the woman in his life. This time the steps he takes to defeat his adversaries feel less like heroic endeavour than steps towards recovery (of masculinity, of patriarchy, of respect). John is doing what men have always done. But it doesn't seem to be working. And he hasn't the patience or the inclination for the long haul. So, he resorts to something else he's done before; as Fred Pfeil notes so tersely in his essay 'From Pillar to Postmodern: Race, Class, and Gender in the Male Rampage Film', he 'runs wild'.[12]

Running wild, Pfeil argues, is at once experiential and metaphorical. It involves a philosophical and actual abandonment of restraint and decorum, an investment in violence as a means to an end *and* as a projection of the hero's, and the collective masculine he epitomises, desperation and frustration at bureaucracy, domestication, Vietnam. Running wild is about breaking rules a rebellion against work, at least the sort of work that has you answering to someone else. It's the Iron John venture out into the woods; face paint, drum and similarly beset buddies in tow. There must be a place where this instinctive behaviour is permitted, where it is appreciated – where this action, this stuff *works*. You'd think that place would be in the action film. But quite bafflingly for John in *Die Hard*, and as we near the end of the American century for the thousands of men who believe in him out there in movieland, it isn't. At least not in and for the long haul.

When John commences running wild, he projects his frustration and shame without having to worry about how Holly might view his actions. She and he are for most of the film necessarily separated by the narrative setting and structure. We abandon the B-story (the marriage melodrama) after the executive washroom scene and don't return to it until just after the hour mark. Through most of the rest of the film, we are asked to ponder how the B-story might be impacted by the A-action film. The answer is, for the most part: less than you think. If you're an Iron John sort of guy: less than you think it should.

Note the spelling of 'Gennero' on the door. It doesn't match the directory

Worth noting: Hans has an easier time than John acknowledging Holly's role as Takagi's second-in-command. They converse as Hans examines the family photo on her desk. He has not yet met John face to face, which is to say he addresses Holly as a married woman, though he does not yet know the identity of her husband. His not-knowing is why we listen closely. 'Mr Takagi has chosen his people well,' Hans intones formally, 'Mrs ...'. Holly, who seems to be forever managing this issue, interrupts and fills in the blank: '*Miss* Gennaro.'

Meantime, John runs wild, oblivious to the B-story he can't understand anyway. Holly occasionally comments on John's antics – 'only John' could drive people so crazy, she muses as another of his stunts frustrates Hans – but the narrative structure that locates him in the A-story exiles her (with him in fact or in mind) in the B. Holly affirms Gennaro over McClane in the B-story not because she's political, but because it keeps both of them safe. He isn't to know this, as he finds curious comfort in the action film that distracts from the domestic melodrama and the romantic comedy aspects of his life.

Whenever John has a moment of respite, he drifts into self-doubt and regret. Such self-pity, an iteration of Bly's notion of 'shame', is in 1980s cinema quintessentially masculine. Let's not

A cop on the edge: Martin Riggs (Mel Gibson) in *Lethal Weapon*

forget, Riggs begins *Lethal Weapon* with a pistol in his mouth. For men like John and Riggs, actions speak louder than words. Being a man as they understand it involves risking death. They put their lives on the line time and again to express a frustration at the seeming failure of the only notion or version of masculinity they can embrace or perform. Riggs's wife is dead. John's is alive but drifting away. The loneliness and despair are debilitating. And both men realise they only have themselves to blame.

John feels beset at every turn, misunderstood at home and on the job. When the FBI cut the power to the building, John remarks to himself aloud, 'I've got a bad feeling about this.' Post-1977, post-*Star Wars*, the allusion is impossible to miss. The phrase likens John to Han Solo, who delivers this same line more than once and in more than one *Star Wars* film. The aptly named Solo and John are cast from the same mould: they are improvisational rogues. 'I've got a bad feeling about this' is what the hero says aloud to himself and to us because he's reached a certain stage in the narrative, a stage – as we share his feelings, his sense of timing – *we* recognise as well. It marks what the script guru Blake Snyder (more on him later) terms the 'dark night of the soul', in which the hero 'hits bottom … mourning the loss of what has [apparently] died, the dream, the goal ... the love of [his] life'.[13] In this moment of reflection, this dark night of the soul, it is only our faith in the hero that has us believing that things are about to turn around again, even if and because the hero is not, for a fleeting moment, so confident they will. We are meant to recognise in this line of dialogue a vulnerability and self-doubt inherent to a peculiar postmodern masculinity ... inherent to a peculiar postmodern moment of metafiction as well.

John is a proper 1980s hero and his concern that the FBI will make things worse coincides with what plenty of filmgoers are thinking at the time: that, per Reagan, bureaucrats and other representatives of big government are part of the problem and not its solution. John gives voice to his feelings of dread because an FBI fuck-up is a plausible endpoint here. (Ironic, then, that this parallels how things will fall apart for McTiernan in Hollywood. More on that later.)

Fearing the worst, John's thoughts shift to the proverbial refrigerator box on the highway. So, he gets on the two-way with Al: 'Tell [Holly] what a jerk I've been ... Tell her she's the best thing that's ever happened to a bum like me. She's heard me say "I love you" a thousand times, but she's never heard me say "I'm sorry".' Al, the ever-loyal sidekick replies: 'You can tell her yourself.' John has voiced his shame here, but not to Holly – to his male buddy instead. A step towards recovery, perhaps. But if it is, he never takes the next step, he never says he's sorry to Holly. Even when he gets the chance at the end of the film. His victory over Hans convinces him that actions speak louder and clearer than words. And he's wrong about that. In 1988, love, to bastardise a Hollywood movie truism, means sometimes you really do have to say you're sorry. And that's a lesson, through this film and three sequels, John will consistently fail to learn.

Holly's identity as a Miss or Mrs (Ms was a thing in 1988 but not an option, apparently, in the film), as a Gennaro or a McClane, is so much at issue throughout the film that some contemporary filmgoers disparage the ending as misogynist or anti-feminist. This ignores the fact that Holly views the name *she chooses*, and

by extension the gender politics implied in that choice, in practical terms. She goes by Gennaro at work not to repudiate the patriarchy or to diminish her attachment to John, but to ease her ascent up the corporate ladder. Takagi knows about John, and he also knows about the kids, who are safely out of the way at home with the housekeeper. The bosses back in Japan have apparently adopted a 'don't ask/don't tell' policy. And Holly sees no upside in rocking their boat.

The children have kept John's surname because it's simpler and easier for them. That Holly uses Gennaro at work and McClane most everywhere else is not a big deal to her. And it shouldn't be a big deal to John. But it is, and that is *his* problem. A lesson *he* needs to learn. And he doesn't. In the sequels, we watch John defeat prodigious enemies: terrorists, master criminals bent on revenge, fellow cops, airport security, the FAA and FBI. But he never gets over himself. And he never will.

The media stumble into *Die Hard* at just past the film's midpoint and make matters worse in both the A- and B-storylines. Reagan's America, again: the media are not to be trusted. At once impulsive and exploitative, the media in *Die Hard* are epitomised by a nightcrawler, an opportunistic and unethical roving reporter named Richard 'Dick' Thornburg (William Atherton). He descends upon Holly's home, bullies the housekeeper and interrogates little Lucy McClane on live TV. Holly's dual identity – the distinction she draws between work and family life – is less about gender than plot structure here, as a tersely edited sequence cinematically reveals. We see Lucy look into a TV camera and say, 'Come home,' and then cut to Holly watching her. Elsewhere such a cool customer, Holly is unable to conceal her reaction to what she's just seen on screen. Her eyes take us to the next shot: Hans figuring out that Holly and John are wife and husband. He picks up the picture on her desk – a picture that's been put down and then propped up a few times in the film – and calls her by her married/family name, 'Mrs McClane'. He will continue to refer to Holly as Mrs McClane from this point on, as her identity is for Hans usefully tied to John's.

Hans takes Holly hostage. As John's wife, she has added value alive. 'McClane' takes her out of the Nakatomi hostage group, to whom she is still Gennaro. This keeps her separate from the group doomed by the explosives set on the roof. The McClane name buys her time. And in an action film, in an action novel like *Nothing Lasts Forever* (as Leland and his daughter tragically realise), timing is everything.

John ascends to the heliport atop the Tower and calls her name – this time: 'Holly Gennaro.' Has he made peace with her dual identity and by extension her career plans as well? Or is he simply

Hans discovers that Holly Gennaro is also Holly McClane

using the name her Nakatomi colleagues will know her by? After he is told that Holly isn't with the rest of the workers, after we know that as Hans's hostage she has become for better or worse Holly McClane, John dutifully shepherds the panicked throng back down the stairs. The problematics of Holly's identity have, as the script had promised early on, brought the A- and B-stories together. John is still fighting terrorists – at least that's what he thinks he is doing. But he is also trying to rescue and reclaim *his* wife. Here, finally, he is doing both at the same time.

John's climactic confrontation with Hans (discussed in more detail in the next chapter) further conflates the two storylines. Much as John has manoeuvred his way to this moment alone, to defeat Hans he will need the help of his other, better half. For John, being a man involves being with Holly. Here, at the film's climax, Holly makes clear she is not 'the kind of girl' meant only to be rescued by the hero – another fact often missed in criticisms of the film. In this climactic moment, she participates actively in the improvisation that sends Hans out of yet another broken window. After *they* kill Hans, Holly and John celebrate their victory with a kiss – a gesture that confirms victory in both the A- and B-storylines, a gesture conspicuously and awkwardly not performed when John first arrived at the Christmas party.

After Hans is dispatched, the film's second ending finds John and Holly arm in arm. Amidst the rubble and busy first responders, Holly looks lovingly at John. John, meantime, is looking elsewhere, looking for someone else. We cut to a subjective shot of what John sees: Al strolling towards them in a variable focus shot. The music swells to accompany this moment of recognition. And it is hard to miss that McTiernan has staged this as a romantic scene. We cut to a three-shot of John, Holly and Al. John smiles in recognition. Al laughs, which has currency here; in the absence of physical intimacy, it's a way men can express mutual affection. Just minutes earlier, John, Hans and Eddie had shared a laugh. They had fought the good fight and begrudgingly expressed a bond as men, as worthy adversaries. Laughter for these adversaries is at once an affirmation of and distancing from. They laugh, recognising together that other expressions of intimacy are not in the playbook.

What follows the shared laughter is one last scene of violence. We see Al and John embrace in the foreground as Holly retreats to the background, politely averting her eyes from an expression of intimacy only men who have been, as they used to say in Vietnam, 'in the shit' can appreciate and understand. Her role in the defeat of Hans and his gang is never acknowledged; for me, a conspicuous

problem with and an inconsistency in this final scene. A second angle on the embrace instructs us on how we might understand John and Al's relationship. The two men are laughing, letting down their guards. They are free to show weakness, homosocial connection. This second shot is blocked awkwardly; Holly is barely in the frame. John chooses this moment to introduce his two partners to each other: 'Al, this is my wife – Holly Gennaro.' He says this without thinking. We can barely see Holly between and behind the two men as she delivers the line that rankles many contemporary filmgoers, correcting John as she shakes Al's hand, affirming her perhaps now undivided self: 'Holly McClane.'

The scene weirdly recalls the denouement of *Rebel Without a Cause* (Nicholas Ray, 1955), when Jim introduces Judy to his father. How the two scenes relate is too complicated to be intended, to be deliberate. But the impact of this late introduction, following scenes of violence as it does in both films, is similarly strange. Is this really what needs to be done here before 'The End' appears on screen and underscored music takes us out of the world of the film? Both Nicholas Ray and John McTiernan apparently think so.

Al, I think significantly, does not react to the remark … which is to say, he does not instruct us on how to react. Instead, he confers his blessing, his best wishes on the potential reconciliation. 'You've got a good man,' he says in a narrow-focus three-shot. Holly is looking at John. John and Al are looking at each other. It's how the scene is blocked and edited, so it's surely intentional. And weird. 'You [Holly] take good care of him,' Al says. We can take this as an affirmation of traditional gender roles and family values or more literally, as John is bloodied and exhausted and rather needs some tender loving care. We don't get a lot of time to ponder the scene, as the mood is broken by Dwayne, who, despite everything that's happened, insists John has things 'to answer for'. It's a ridiculous position to take, a comic exaggeration of a middle manager, an officious administrator. John has won the day *because* he rejected proper police procedure. Because, instead of working with Dwayne, he put on his face paint and banged his drum. Because he ran wild.

The conversation with Dwayne ends abruptly, before John has time to respond. The sudden sound of the crowd shouting cues the amazing resurrection of Karl, presumed dead, gun drawn and aimed at John. Al's role in John's life shifts back to the professional – it has to, really. These are men, after all. And whatever is transpiring between them is too emotional to go on much longer. Al draws his gun and kills Karl, making possible the reconciliation of John and Holly, the B-storyline that even at this late point still needs some working out. Thanks to Al, John and Holly are finally free to leave the Christmas party where she has been Holly Gennaro, in a limousine that will take them home, where she and the kids have always been McClanes.

Argyle's late arrival provides something of a kick-in-the-pants, comic third ending. The sight of his limo hurtling into Nakatomi Plaza offers comic relief *and* a bit of structural symmetry. At the start of the film John is uncomfortable with the limo pick-up. The luxury car is a metaphor for Holly's posh LA existence, a reminder of her lofty professional standing. John is not a limo kind of guy, so he sits in the front seat. Here at the end, without thinking, he gets in the back seat with Holly. And they kiss. Like teenagers, like young lovers do. And though this is hardly on their minds at the time, they prepare to navigate the awful traffic that awaits them like proper LA executives do, without having to get behind the wheel. They prepare to navigate their relationship as well, elated at John's victory and temporarily distracted from the problems neither has done anything to solve.

Hans has warned John that he won't live to ride off into the sunset with Grace Kelly. But in an important way, John gets *his High Noon* ending and rides off in style. Will Kane, the Gary Cooper character in *High Noon* (Fred Zinnemann, 1952), gets to the denouement in his film his way, on his terms. He has put his personal relationship with his pacifist, Quaker wife, played by the

ever-luminous Grace Kelly, on hold, and has risked his marriage's dissolution, insisting upon getting the dirty work of law enforcement out of the way first. John, too, has survived some dirty business and is free here at the end to make whatever he can out of a second chance at married life. But it's 1988, not 1952. And John's not ready to retire to the quiet life on a ranch. Neither, it is worth adding, is Holly.

John's seeming comfort in the back seat of Argyle's limo offers hope that he and Holly might make it work this time. It implies as well that John may be staying in LA for a while – a plot point picked up in the sequel, *Die Hard 2* (Renny Harlin, 1990), then dismissed as impossible in the later instalments of the franchise. The happy ending in *Die Hard* is at best provisional, debatable, a reminder that he's only put off what he failed to do in the executive washroom scene. *Die Hard*, as it was conceived by its screenwriter Jeb Stuart, is about a man who needs to apologise. John does a lot of things in *Die Hard*. But an apology isn't one of them.

## **3** The Whammy Theory

The choice of McTiernan to direct *Die Hard* built upon the surprising
success of his sci-fi-action picture *Predator*, produced the year before
*Die Hard* by Lawrence Gordon and Joel Silver for Fox. The film is
about an elite band of American military veterans sent by the CIA to
a Central American jungle to rescue survivors of a helicopter crash
(or so they are told). The band's leader, Dutch Schaefer (played by
Arnold Schwarzenegger), takes on this mercenary work to confront
and surmount his post-Vietnam anomie, but instead revisits the
crimes of the past as the mission becomes a lot more complicated
and a lot more dangerous than advertised. Dutch was modelled after
Sylvester Stallone's John Rambo, and his deployment to this other
faraway, godforsaken jungle (the film was, for the record, shot in

Arnold Schwarzenegger with fellow hard body Carl Weathers in a publicity
still for *Predator* (1987)

Mexico) leads to an encounter with a prodigious opponent: an alien that takes to hunting him. Objectives, we are reminded here, are never so clear after Vietnam – the federal government, our leaders, are still (as ever) not to be trusted. The alien awaiting Dutch and his gang in the jungle is technologically and physically superior, typical of the upside-down world of post-Vietnam action films, in which US special forces (and they are all in these films *special*) find themselves outmanned and outgunned.

The screenwriters Jim and John Thomas wrote Dutch with Stallone in mind. But not exactly or only because of Rambo. Their initial inspiration was a joke circulating around Hollywood at the time that, after *Rocky IV* (Sylvester Stallone, 1985), in which the rust-belt striver defeats a bigger, stronger Russian fighter named Ivan Drago, *Rocky V* would involve a fight with an extraterrestrial. For the Thomases, *Predator* was *Rocky*, but in a jungle, with aliens.[14]

The production team for *Die Hard* embraced the sociopolitical matrices of *Rocky*, *Rambo* and *Predator*, developing a variation on a theme that had been successfully explored before. John ventures into a strange foreign landscape and, despite being outgunned, commits to an armed conflict that – after Vietnam, and against all odds – he believes, like Rambo, like Dutch, he can win this time.

At the start of the film, from the front seat of Argyle's limousine, John finds the southland sprawl disorienting, a feeling made worse when he, a working-class cop, enters the glittering new corporate high-rise where Holly works. The Klaxon Oil skyscraper from Thorp's novel is in *Die Hard* the American headquarters for a Japanese firm, Nakatomi. The building bears the Japanese company's name, a reminder of the dubious state of American industry in 1988. John's adversaries are from out of town too, and, after Vietnam, they have become accustomed to pushing America around.

The skyscraper featured in the film's exteriors is Fox Plaza, a 34-storey, 493-foot tower at 2121 Avenue of the Stars in Century City, built in part to house business offices for the film studio distributing the film. The poster the studio used to support the

Our first sight of the Nakatomi (Fox) Plaza from Argyle's limo

release included a rendering of the building in an explicit reference to the 1974 disaster film *The Towering Inferno*, directed by John Guillermin, and also distributed by Fox. The commercial building was barely a year old in 1988 and these early images showed it already tumbling down.

Designed by Scott Johnson for the firm Johnson Fain, Fox Plaza was very 1980s postmodern, with a Hotel Bonaventure-like atrium interior, a pink granite and tinted-glass exterior, and an unexpected and somewhat implausible church spire at its apex (it is a building meant for business, after all, not for prayer). The structure was meant to stand out against the more traditionally modernist Century City skyline, as it surely drew from Robert Venturi, Denise Scott Brown and Steven Izenour's 1972 postmodern playbook, *Learning from Las Vegas*. Its style implied a Los Angeles nowhere city – an architecture evinced not by and remarkable not to passers-by on foot (as no one walks in LA) but to drivers passing by in their cars,[15] an architecture and larger cultural style that embodied, according to Fredric Jameson, 'the logic of late capitalism'.[16] Ronald Reagan housed his post-presidential offices at Fox Plaza, on the 34th floor, not far from the site of the action in the film. The building later featured in a few other Hollywood films, most famously at the end of *Fight Club* (David Fincher, 1999) – there, too, with a nod and a wink to Venturi et al., Jameson et al. The Fox is one of the buildings destroyed during Project Mayhem, as the male panic terrorists target the American credit industry.[17]

In *Die Hard*'s climactic scene atop the Nakatomi Plaza, John finally discovers that the terrorists aren't terrorists. When he remarks on this discovery aloud, he affirms his place among so many other post-Vietnam heroes, realising he has risked his life for a cause that, even in victory, will be diminished in the public's view. John fights his war on two fronts – the enemies foreign (the gang) and domestic (the LAPD hostage negotiator Dwayne Robinson, the FBI agents who arrive late to the scene and the 24-hour news media). Rambo wants a war he can win. John too. And even when and as they do – win, that is – they are asked to account for a breach of protocol, for a libertarian resistance to the regulatory matrix of big government epitomised by Dwayne's dumbass insistence on a debrief at the very moment our hero, John, has earned a make-out session in the back of a limousine.

In the absence of the box-office appeal of a Schwarzenegger or Stallone, the *Die Hard* production team had a lot riding on Bruce Willis's move from small to big screen, this at a time when that transition was not as easy as it is today. Unlike the era's other hard bodies, those barely articulate, well-muscled heroes, Willis offered by way of variation a hero we might more easily relate to: hairy, barrel-chested, funny. Willis's self-effacing asides make cheeky allusion to his wise-cracking character on *Moonlighting*. The asides are as well a necessary quirk of the screenplay, since he is often alone in the film. John's penchant for talking to himself positions us as his accomplices and confidantes. He is our kind of wild friend with whom tonight we might get into a little trouble. And we like him for that. Willis's easy charm suited the role.

*Die Hard* was doubly rooted in TV: the aforementioned *Moonlighting* and *MacGyver*, a popular show that ran from 1985 to 1992. *MacGyver* featured the physically unremarkable Richard Dean Anderson as a New Age mercenary whose talents lay in improvisation, utilising what he has or finds at hand to solve a complicated problem. Anderson, like Willis, and unlike the outrageous hard-body stars Stallone and Schwarzenegger, invited identification, not idealisation. *MacGyver* was so popular that the eponymous character's surname found its way into the American vernacular as a verb. To 'MacGyver' something meant to transform or jury-rig. Plenty of filmgoers watching *Die Hard* in 1988 appreciated that John's improvisations resembled those performed by the TV hero.

John, like MacGyver, revels in his role as the 'fly in the ointment'. There is throughout something attractively adolescent about his shenanigans, flurries of activity that never last long enough to be boring and leave behind a mess he has no intention of cleaning up. He is naughty by nature, battling pretension, regiment, protocol. We root for John much as we root for Dennis the Menace or Kevin from *Home Alone* (Chris Columbus, 1990), Joel from *Risky Business* (Paul Brickman, 1983) or Ferris Bueller: naughty boys who outsmart adults who underestimate their ingenuity, their penchant for destruction, their survival instincts.

For example: after the chair bomb detonates, the device a MacGyvered piece of office furniture, John ponders his handiwork. He asks Al if the building is on fire, if his stunt maybe went a bit too far. Al reassures him. There's plenty of damage all right – Nakatomi Tower will need 'a paint job and a shitload of screen doors' – the sort of repairs some dumb stunt performed by Dennis or Kevin or Joel or Ferris might require. At the end of the film, the Tower will in fact require much more than a coat of paint and some new hardware; witness the dozens of first responders. Dwayne holds John responsible for the mess. And that is why we find Dwayne humourless and comically stupid. When the Ferrari ends up in the drink in *Ferris Bueller's Day Off* (John Hughes, 1986), we laugh because only a killjoy (and the car's unlikable owner) would hold Ferris and his friends to account. We laugh, those of us in the know at least, because no actual or real Ferraris were harmed in the making of the film.[18]

When Thornburg witnesses the chair bomb explosion, he is unaware of its source or John's role in the developing drama. Rather than express concern for lives possibly lost and property damage caused, Thornburg looks to his cameraman and says, 'Tell me you got that.' Assured that the footage has been captured, he muses aloud, 'Eat your heart out Channel Five.' The footage is valuable only as far as it helps him, only as far as it helps one news outfit and not another. It is important to add here that most of the news reporting is incorrect. The reporters assume they are covering 'a terrorist takeover of the Nakatomi building' and use footage to suit that narrative. They, too, are bound to be disappointed when they discover that Hans is not a terrorist … that the story they have been following so sensationally is just a robbery.

Interesting, then, to ponder the same risk taken by the film-makers. They promise in the trailer and in the opening thirty minutes a film about terrorists, based on a novel about terrorists, at the very moment international terrorism is on everyone's mind (including Hollywood's: see, for example, John Frankenheimer's *Black Sunday*, a 1977 action film inspired by the terrorist attack during the 1972 Munich Olympics). And what they deliver instead is a heist picture. This is why the special effects are so important, and why the film is less the sum of story elements than of things that go boom in the night. Whammies. The term sounds suitably childish or childlike. But these are films made by and for oversized children, for men (mostly) and women who defiantly won't grow up.

In a 1991 article for *Esquire* magazine, the scriptwriter and novelist John Gregory Dunne recalls the first time he encountered what would come to be regarded in Hollywood as 'the Whammy Theory':

Meeting: Not long ago. We [Dunne and his wife and co-writer Joan Didion] were asked to rewrite a caper thriller about a bank robbery that takes place during a hurricane ... We were told that what the producers wanted was a combination of *Key Largo* and *Die Hard*; we were to provide the *Key Largo* element ... Speaking of the script, [we asked] how did [the producer] see the first act? 'Better whammies,' he said. Whammies we had been told were special effects that killed a lot of people, and that it was this season's theory, formulated by a producer named Joel Silver and known as the Joel Silver Whammy Theory, that a whammy had to occur every ten minutes to keep the attention of the audience. 'What then do we do about the second act?' 'Second act, whammies mount up.' ... whammies mount up, I later realized, is the contemporary equivalent of 'complications ensue' ... 'Third act?' 'All whammies.'[19]

Thanks to Silver and his whammy theory, today one finds at most every studio screening a mid-level manager manning a stopwatch, caring less about what they see than when they see it. The whammy theory presages the current screenwriters' bible, Blake Snyder's *Save the Cat!* (2005), a plug-and-play template for the modern American movie script similarly built upon sequential beats. The specifics of the Snyder template are less important than what its programmatic structure implies: that film scripts share a common pattern and that variations are meant to fit into the formula, not to depart from it. Most important: film stories transpire in actual time, in time passing. A successful script, Snyder contends, moves in beats through a set sequence of events or screenwriting tasks – 'opening image, set-up, theme stated, catalyst, debate, break into two, B story, the promise of the premise, midpoint, bad guys close in, all is lost, dark night of the soul, break into three, finale, final image' – always with an eye on the clock, attention paid to things starting and quickly finishing.[20]

In *Die Hard*, there is from start to finish a barrelling forward in a single locale, as if multiple settings might take too much time, might require a time-wasting transition or two. We see vehicles arriving – the limo, the van, the cops, the news truck, a Humvee, a helicopter – but, once John is at the site, McTiernan never cutting away to their site of origin. There are no flashbacks. Duration is the key here: time just for things to happen, to unfold – time spent in the theatre, time as experience of immersion, of engagement, of being on the edge of one's seat. There is no sense of 'later that day'. No sense of later, at least, until we get there. The past exists, but mostly as something discredited, dispatched, disregarded. Hans was a terrorist but now he's a thief. Holly was a McClane but now she's a Gennaro (at least some of the time). John was in New York. Now he's in LA. He was a husband and a father but now he's not sure what role he has in Holly's world. Time in *Die Hard* is always moving forward and fast. The film never veers from this propulsive chronology.

The whammy theory is reductive, albeit less dogmatic or programmatic than Snyder's formula, as all whammies are basically the same. To break *Die Hard* down as a film, we need only track the whammies. That's certainly how the film was broken down by its production team and engineered to fit Silver's formula. The breakdown that follows reveals the film's essential beat structure, its organisation built upon production numbers, like in a musical, or sex scenes in pornography.

There are, by my count, seventeen whammies in *Die Hard*. Counting whammies is not an exact science, mind you. The first comes seventeen minutes in – late, comparatively, for the genre, following the film's initial gestures at genres (melodrama and romantic comedy) not so suited to the whammy structure. The final whammy highlights the coda, the film's second ending at 2 hours and 5 minutes in. For reference: the film's listed running time is 2 hours and 12 minutes.[21]

## Whammy 1 (17 minutes in)

Theo and Karl walk briskly into the Nakatomi Tower lobby and approach the front desk, an entrance punctuated by the film's first whammy as Karl kills the security guard. Theo gets on the two-way radio and gets things rolling: 'We're in'. Theo mans the console to

disable the security system. Hans arrives moments later; we know he is the gang's leader without being told. A sequence of shots signals simultaneity: the elevator en route to the 30th floor / the gang inside cocking their weapons / a slow zoom-in on Hans that prompts / a medium close-up of John anxious at losing his connection, prefacing the off-screen sound of machine-gun fire and a woman's scream. This A-story hook introduces the setting, principal characters and stakes of the film. Whammies, in 1988, are narrative.

## Whammy 2 (31 minutes in)

A second cold-blooded killing as Takagi refuses to give up the combination to the safe. One body per whammy. One whammy at a time. So far at least. As whammies go, this one comes and goes quickly. Still, it has a singular impact.

## Whammy 3 (36 minutes in)

John sets off a fire alarm as a prank. What's he up to? We're not sure. The action has the unintended effect of revealing his location to Hans, who dispatches Tony. Tony thinks he's got the drop on John and says, 'You might as well come out and join the others.' But John isn't one of the others. John gets the better of Tony and seizes his weapon.

Tony is polite to John. John is impolite in return. He calls Tony 'a dickhead'. A subtext throughout is that polity is a mode or aspect of dishonesty. John identifies himself as a cop. Tony reasons: 'You won't hurt me. You're a policeman and there are rules for policemen.' He's right, but being right will do him no good. A fair fight ensues, ending when a fall down the stairs kills Tony. John's hands are clean, sort of, and only for the time being.

### Whammy 4 (40 minutes in)

Building upon the previous fight scene, John steals Tony's shoes but they don't fit. 'Nine million terrorists in the world and I gotta kill one with feet smaller than my sister's.' It is a comment about manhood, shoe size and whatever else that might relate to. John outfits Tony for maximum snark-effect and sends him back to Hans like some damaged Christmas present, returned for exchange. The defiled dead body sets in motion a subplot involving John and Karl, as we discover that the somewhat hapless Tony was the not-at-all hapless Karl's brother. When Karl encounters his brother's risibly rendered corpse, he overturns a desk and shouts, 'I want blood.' It's a promise he will make good on in Whammy 11, and again in Whammy 17. Interesting here again: the whammy is an expression of plot and not, or not just, a jolting beat in the rhythm of the film.

### Whammy 5 (45 minutes in)

We are now officially in the 'whammies mount' period of what we used
to call Act 2, as a full seven minutes of gunfire ensue, involving plenty
of broken glass – a realistic detail, perhaps, but also a foreshadowing
of a later scene in which the gang, who are astonishingly poor
marksmen, stop trying to shoot John and simply shoot at glass
partitions they can't possibly miss to bloody John's bare feet.

### Whammy 6 (55 minutes in)

We cut away from the noise and action to find Al, quietly loading up
on Twinkies. We must come up for air sometime. Al tells the clerk the
unhealthy snack cakes are for his pregnant wife, but the explanation,
true as it may be, doesn't fly. This comic scene is not set at Nakatomi
Plaza, a rarity. It feels at first like exposition, so maybe it's time to
hit the concession stand. But we will need to be quick about it, as
Al will in a few minutes take on the role of the sweet-natured Black
action-film sidekick – after *Lethal Weapon*, a Joel Silver trope. Al is
introduced as a pudgy soft body in an ill-fitting uniform, waddling his
way into a film that has up to this moment seen its fair share of harder
bodies. The implication is: Al is all John gets when he calls for help.

John has called police dispatch on a secure channel, but as will
characterise the *Die Hard* franchise, such calls for administrative help

are met with disbelief and distrust. The ideological state apparatus – I am dating myself here, I know, but Althusser was surely relevant still in 1988 – is dysfunctional and incompetent.[22] The bureaucrat in charge admonishes John for not following protocol. She suspects the call is a prank, but dispatches Al to drive by the Tower just in case John's legit. Ironic, then, as that too is protocol, a matter of procedure that is less about efficiency than plausible deniability. Al dutifully does his drive-by and then enters the building to check in with Eddie, whom he mistakes for the building concierge. (Key here: We know that Eddie is a gang member. Al does not.) We cut away from this quiet scene to a far noisier whammy dozens of floors above. More gunfire. And this time a bullet hits its target. And then another. John deftly fires up through a table. As if getting shot, getting killed, isn't indignity enough, we can easily guess where the bullet strikes its target. Getting it in the bollocks is always funny.

Back to Al thirty floors below. He hasn't heard a thing. That's funny too. Al exits the Tower satisfied that all's well. Whammy 6 has come and gone without him. He ambles back to his patrol car singing 'Let It Snow! Let It Snow! Let It Snow!', a Christmas standard. But he can't quite remember the words.

### Whammy 7 (57 minutes in)

Al calls in to dispatch to say, 'That's a wild goose chase over here at Nakatomi Plaza.' But just as he puts his car in gear, a body, a gang member John has just killed, crashes down onto his squad car. Al freaks out. This initially distinguishes him from John, who it seems (by inference) has seen his share of killing. Al has, too, but we don't know that yet. The real difference between the two men is that gun violence still has meaning for Al. We're not to know that either. Later, it will be hard to resist thinking that Al's freak-out is a necessary stage – the pudgy Al stage – in becoming John, a hard-body *man* of action. John will not become Al at the end of the film. But Al, the Twinkie-hoarding cop in uniform – and we wonder, is he us? – will become John. We will need to wait for Whammy 17 for that.

The sound and sight of the body hitting the car cues gunfire from the gang inside. Al puts the car in reverse and backs out of the line of fire, revealing, for comic relief, that he's a terrible driver. He and John will share a laugh about this later, and that will further cement their bond. Al drives in reverse past Argyle, who is in the garage on the car phone (in 1988, a luxury), music blasting – another bit of comic relief.

Al is still the no-action Al. And Argyle is just a wiseacre limo driver. Argyle's comic cluelessness is initially presented in counterpoint to the efficient computer genius and safe-cracker Theo. This proves to be another misdirection as later in the film Argyle thwarts Theo's escape, an intervention that reverses the initial dynamic; Theo, the uber-confident Black tech genius, is in the end foiled by the (only seemingly) feckless working-class temp driver, just as the classically educated Hans is outwitted and outfought by John, a working-class cop benumbed by American TV and movie Westerns.

Al calls in with the bad news about bodies falling from the sky. The cops arrive in haste and all at once. The media, too, as they monitor police channels. John will from here on struggle against the thieves he still thinks are terrorists, bumbling government bureaucrats from the LAPD and FBI, and the 24-hour media, all the while knowing that, win or lose, no one will thank him for his service.

At the risk of being a killjoy, films built on whammies generally involve plenty of gunfire, and as such may well desensitise filmgoers to gun violence. Whether this extends past the lights coming up and to a larger desensitisation to gun violence in America, the real place where real guns kill real people, is a harder, larger question. As an intellectual, I resist the notion that filmgoers can't recognise the difference between movies and real life. But as an American for whom gun violence has on occasion come close to home, I am not so sure.[23]

## Whammy 8 (1 hour and 13 minutes in)

The SWAT team arrives and lays siege to the Tower. They are easily repelled by the gang. We see an armoured Humvee make its way to the front entrance. The film-makers are on to something here. A fact of post-Vietnam police work is the repurposing of Vietnam-era military hardware. Intercut with the Humvee approach, we see the gang set up a rocket launcher. Seems they have their surplus outlet too. Important here: Hans has come prepared for the SWAT team assault. He has expected it. As he told Takagi, he's all into details, preparedness.

We hear on the soundtrack Theo offering what sounds like TV commentary on an American football game. When the rocket

impacts and blows the Humvee out of commission, he shouts: 'The quarterback's toast.' We cut to the cops, caught by surprise at the gang's armoury and skill. Then back to Hans: 'Hit it again.'

## Whammy 9 (1 hour and 15 minutes in)

John 'MacGyvers' a desk chair with explosives. The detonation blows out the windows on a lower floor and the fireball comes back up the elevator shaft and nearly takes him out too. The two explosions (Whammies 8 and 9) characterise the players involved: Hans brings equipment he then employs with expertise. John finds the plastique

and improvises a bomb that makes a lot of noise, causes property damage and nearly kills him too.

## Whammy 10 (1 hour and 35 minutes in)

We wait a while for this next whammy, and when we get to it, it's just a tease. Hans wanders off by himself into a section of the Tower still under construction, where John stumbles upon him. To explore more closely, Hans has stupidly left his flashlight and gun on a ledge. The camera lingers on this brief lapse in judgement. It's too easy, too early to be the final confrontation. Still, we know some sort of whammy is at hand.

When John gets the drop on Hans, we wonder: how will this not go John's way? We get some time to think about the situation as we cut away to a little comic relief played out between the FBI and LAPD, between the imperious Agents Johnson and the eager to please Dwayne. McTiernan is playing with time. We cut back as Hans tries to trick John into thinking he is a Nakatomi employee hiding out of sight. The London-born Rickman playing a German ex-terrorist here adopts a terrible American accent – an accent so bad, and from such a good actor, it has got to be bad on purpose. Hans introduces himself as Bill Clay, a name pulled from the directory. At first, John appears fooled by the improvisation. The two men bond over John's last two cigarettes. Even here, John, who knows (though we don't know that he knows) that Bill is Hans, is generous. A good guy. 'You know how to use a handgun, Bill?' John asks. 'Bill' says he played paintball once on a company retreat. John hands 'Bill' what we assume to be a loaded gun. 'Time for the real thing, Bill.'

Hans gets on the two-way and shifts easily away from American-accented English to German. We see John register that Bill is not what he seems. So why, then, is John smiling? 'Always the cowboy …?' Maybe, but he's also nobody's fool. 'You should be on fuckin' TV with that accent,' he says. Hans pulls the trigger. We hear a click but no pop. 'No bullets.' John says, 'You think I'm stupid, Hans?' The answer is there in the asking. Whatever John plans to do

with Hans is interrupted by a proper whammy: click *and* pop. The
elevator door opens, and a gunfight ensues.

Dozens of bullets are fired and again, astonishingly, none hit
their target. Hans has made a mental note of John's bare feet and
says to Karl: '*Schieß den Fenster!*' (It sounds like '*Schieß dem
Fenster!*' but that must be a mispronunciation.) Karl looks back at
him befuddled. Hans repeats the line, this time in English: 'Shoot
the glass.' And Karl complies. The exchange is innocuous, but it
encourages a question or two. In fact, there's a Reddit debate focused
on this line of dialogue.[24]

McTiernan eschews subtitles throughout. The order Hans (a British actor playing a German) gives Karl (a Russian former ballet dancer playing a German) is not how a native speaker would say 'Shoot the glass.' More like, 'Shoot the window.' And even that's not exactly right. That Hans uses the word for window instead of glass may speak to lazy script or continuity work during production, a carelessness characteristic of Hollywood and, in general, American ethnocentrism and isolationism – the very reasons Hans disdains John as an ignorant cowboy. But maybe there's more to this. That Karl doesn't understand the order raises a different or additional question. Is he not German? Was he never a Volksfrei/Baader–Meinhof gang member?

'*Schieß den Fenster*' is a schoolboy mistake. The vocabulary and usage are both off. What Hans should have said is '*Schieß auf das Glas*.' Shoot onto or into the glass. The words for glass and window are not interchangeable. Things are moving forward and fast here. It's a whammy, after all. So, why then call attention to the mistake by cutting to Karl's quizzical look and Hans repeating the line in English? The English translation is not necessary for us, as the order has the desired effect. The gang shatter the glass and John's feet are cut.

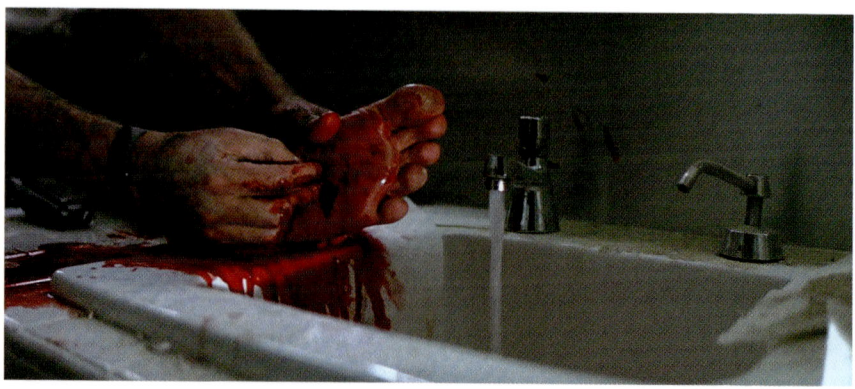

McTiernan is fond here and elsewhere of an immersive visual technique: guns fired directly at the camera, the fast film capturing and/or special visual effects simulating the flash of gunfire. Here the flash amidst dust and smoke lends cover to John's exit. Now he's there; now he isn't. In his haste, John leaves behind the detonators. Whammy 10 took a while in coming but it deposits a prop that serves plot development. Whatever we make of '*Schieß den Fenster*', John's exit without the detonators feels a bit like Hans leaving his gun and flashlight on a ledge. We know this will mean something – that something will be made of this. We just don't know what, yet.

### Whammy 11 (1 hour and 48 minutes in)

Karl runs wild, seeking revenge. We knew this was coming. John v. Karl – fellow hard bodies, fellow gunslingers. Karl is the more adept, the better-trained fighter. But as we should know by now, in the film and in the action genre, John's persistence and ability to take a punch factor significantly: think Rocky v. Apollo Creed, or more usefully (considering outcomes), Rocky v. Ivan Drago. John taunts Karl about his dead brother. It's a curious thing for a hero to do – to gloat over a killing. But it's 1988, and plenty of Americans are tired of getting pushed around. In 1988, the taunt prompted applause. Ever ingenious and a little bit lucky, John, in another instance of

MacGyvering, finally ensnares Karl in a dangling chain and sends him flying across the room into a cement wall.

## Whammy 12 (1 hour and 53 minutes in)

Uli, a gang member, opens a door and John, just seconds after vanquishing Karl, is on the other side of it. John shoots first, asks questions later … and Uli is dead. John ascends to the roof and tries to get the hostages' attention by firing his gun into the air. He needs to get them off the roof as it is rigged to blow up. John wants to help the hostages. He wants to find and help Holly even more. He calls out her name: 'Holly Gennaro.' It's the name the other hostages know her by. It's her work name.

## Whammy 13 (1 hour and 55 minutes in)

The FBI mistake John for a terrorist. He is firing his weapon into the sky, after all. In modern warfare, and perhaps this is the point here, it is difficult to tell who's who. The feds open fire on the roof, risking collateral damage, causing panic and complicating John's efforts to lead the hostages away from danger. John once again magically dodges the bullets. This sort of stunt proliferates the action film and defies physics and reality. We know that, but mostly don't care. Killing in movies can't be easy, even as in reality it is.

John gets the hostages to follow him down the stairs, in part because Agents Johnson are shooting at them too. Interesting how much of this film is logistical. When Hans seizes the office floor early in the film, John ascends to higher ground to watch and wait. Throughout the film, John uses vacant elevator shafts to travel vertically. He hides out in spaces that offer plenty of cover from horizontal ambush. In this scene, he takes the stairs to lead the hostages down from the roof. They hurry past the camera. We see what we presume is Karl's corpse dangling above them. There is no indication that any of the hostages see him. The camera position makes sure we do. McTiernan isn't playing fair here. He shows us Karl dead, only to reveal later that he's not.

## Whammy 14 (1 hour and 56 minutes in)

One of the film's most exhilarating edited sequences – a fifteen-stage action-edited set piece, as McTiernan amps up the pace, cutting to and from multiple camera angles:

1. John leaps out of a window secured by a fire hose
2. A tilt as we eye the detonator plunger and then see Hans as he sets off the charges
3. White Agent Jackson takes aim at John

4. John goes airborne

5. Hans's hands are now on the plunger

6. John aloft, again, still

7. An explosion – cues a flash of light and smoke as John descends

8. A high-angle long shot as the rooftop blows

9. A flat, 90-degree extreme long shot of the rooftop explosion against the night sky

10. The bewildered cops (whatever's happened has happened without them, again – in the modern heroic model, pretty much every affirmative action leaves the cops baffled, panicked, insulted)

11. A high-angle shot of John in relief against the night sky; he is dangling alongside the astonishingly tall building

12. A second angle of John

13. A low angle of the building exploding

14. John dangling on the outside figuring out a way back in, his bloody feet slamming against the window once, then again, then …

15. John shoots out the window – '*Schieß auf das Fenster*' for real this time – and he moves from outside in, in more ways than one.

Shot 4 in the sequence: John goes airborne

Shot 11 in the sequence: a high-angle shot of John in relief against the night sky

The whammy culminates as John perilously wriggles out of the fire hose just before it drags him, along with the hose assembly, back out of the window. It's Act 3, all whammies now, per the formula. McTiernan uses this last stunt with the fire hose to execute a neat bit of foreshadowing. Soon enough Hans will be dangling out of a window, tenuously and alarmingly attached to Holly – an allusion to the climax of *Nothing Lasts Forever* few filmgoers (as most have not read the book) will recognise.

## Whammy 15 (1 hour and 57 minutes in)

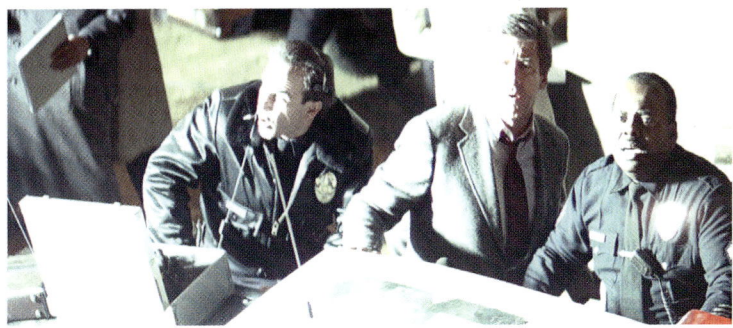

The roof detonation sends a helicopter into a spin. If Dwayne had been more on the ball, if he wasn't such a sycophant, he'd take pleasure in this. Agents Johnson have treated him disrespectfully, after all. But he instead remarks blankly, 'We're gonna need some more FBI guys, I guess.' It plays as comic relief. McTiernan doesn't worry about mixing terror and pleasure, suspense and comedy. All jokes are mean. Why pretend they're not.

## Whammy 16 (2 hours and 1 minute in)

The first of two endings. The A- and B-storylines converge as John seizes the opportunity to take care of the terrorist and estranged marriage plots in one swift action, and with his last two bullets at that. The bearer bonds fall to the floor, and we hear John call out from off screen: 'Hans?' John emerges from the dust and smoke, walking into the frame, arrestingly backlit. He's got a gun at his waist and walks towards the camera in a neatly framed medium close-up as a single sustained chord plays on the soundtrack. We cut to a three-shot of what he sees and then a high-angle four-shot from behind: Hans, Holly and Eddie looking back at John. 'That's what this was about, a fucking robbery?' John finally discovers what we have known for well over an hour. Hans puts a gun to Holly's temple and intones, 'Put down the gun.' We know something Hans doesn't know. That John's gun is empty.

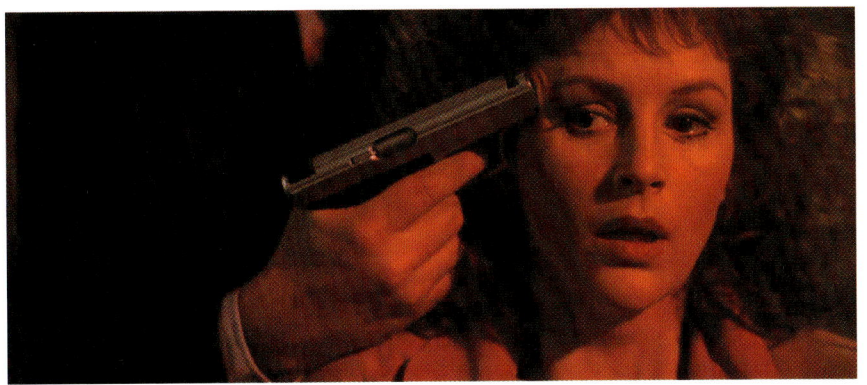

John needs some things explained. Hans, who has displayed little patience with Takagi and Ellis, complies.

JOHN    Why'd you have to nuke the whole building?
HANS    When you steal $600, you can disappear. When you steal $600 million, they will find you unless they think you're already dead.

We cut to a close-up of Holly. Though there's a gun to her head, she remains composed.

She gives John what looks like a signal. We see that John sees it. And that Hans does not. John drops the gun, which cues Eddie to pick up his. Hans isn't done talking. He tells Eddie, 'Nein, this is mine.' John puts his hands behind his head – a performance of supplication that affirms Hans's view of John as an American drama queen. We see John in low angle. He looms large. The visual language is clear to us (and not to Hans): this is not a surrender. John says, 'You got me.' But we know Hans does not.

McTiernan holds on John as Hans begins, off screen: 'Still the cowboy, Mr McClane, Americans all alike. Well, this time John Wayne does not walk off into the sunset with Grace Kelly.' Hans has got the *High Noon* co-stars wrong. 'It's Gary Cooper, asshole.' We cut to an oddly framed shot: Rickman/Hans is considerably taller than Bedelia/Holly, so this medium close-up of Rickman cuts off half of Bedelia's face, everything below her eyes. The conversation continues. Why, suddenly, is Hans not in a hurry? We cut to a close-up of Holly. Her eyes tell us she is tuning in to whatever John is up to. The sort of thing married couples do. We cut back to the oddly framed shot of Hans and Holly. The camera placement anticipates her next move; she seems already to be ducking out. Gun at the ready, Hans recalls John's off-colour comment. 'What was it?' he asks for confirmation. 'Yippee-ki-yay motherfuck …'. John laughs, we think at Hans's clunky, accented delivery. The laughter spreads to Hans and Eddie. The camera pans down from just above John's head to find the Season's Greetings Christmas tape and the handgun it holds in place.

Whammy 16 begins and ends quickly: a seconds-long gunfight that John wins with his last two bullets. Having won the day, John blows imaginary smoke off the barrel end of his pistol. The scene's payoff line – 'Happy trails, Hans' – refers to John's earlier aka, 'another cowboy', Roy Rogers.[25] Hans falls backwards out of the window, gun still drawn. He pauses, or so it seems thanks to some slow-motion FX, and remains attached to Holly by an expensive watch she conspicuously sports. The watch signifies her corporate sell-out, or at least her corporate status. The shot is Hitchcockian by intention, with *North by Northwest* (1959) only the most obvious point of reference.

We cut outside to Dwayne and more comic relief: 'Oh, I hope that's not a hostage.' Then back to John and Holly as they kiss. *North by Northwest* again. Two hours earlier, when John arrived after months of separation, the reunion found both Holly and John guarded. Just an awkward moment in which two ex-lovers valued saving face over showing the other how they (still) feel. After all they've been through in the last two hours, they kiss hungrily, appreciating that any time together is precious.

### Whammy 17 (2 hours and 5 minutes in)

John introduces Holly to Al and fields Dwayne's ridiculous demands for a debrief. A disdain for authority is essential to John's running-wild hero. Karl's sudden emergence from the flurry of activity in the devastated Nakatomi Plaza prevents John from doing something stupid, something so insubordinate and impolitic he might not escape the consequences. The sound of the crowd around them shouting cues Karl's entrance. John freezes in open-mouthed surprise, then instinctively tackles Holly to protect her body with his own. Being instinctively protective has never been the problem.

We see Karl screen left in a medium close-up, automatic weapon at the ready. Then a pistol. We know it's not John's gun. He's on the ground. And it's not Karl's either; he's at the other end

of the frame with a different firearm. The bullet hits Karl. Blood
explodes from the wound and he falls backwards. A second bullet is
fired as McTiernan cuts from the flash at the gun's barrel to evidence
of a bullet hitting its target. We then cut to John in a choker close-up,
his eyes wide open in fear and surprise. The look instructs us. John
has seen a lot coming that we wouldn't have. What has surprised us
here has surprised him too. Karl falls backwards, prompting a cut to
a low-angle close-up of Al's gun, centre of the frame, pointing at the
camera, an allusion to yet another movie Western, *The Great Train
Robbery* (Edwin S. Porter, 1903), which famously ends with Bronco
Billy Anderson discharging his pistol into the camera, a gesture aimed
figuratively if not also literally at the filmgoer, at us. Here a brief
vertical camera move, a tilt most likely, accompanies a rack focus that
takes us from the gun to its holder, Al, a look of grim determination
on his face.

The film's final whammy caps the action, leaving little time for a
proper denouement, what we used to call the anticlimax, not because
it operates against the climax but because it is not in and of itself
climactic. John and Holly get into the back seat of Argyle's limo to
do what lovers do. John is not going to Pomona. He's probably not
going to have to sleep in the guest room. He's earned his way back
into her arms and into her bed.

Holly and John's marriage has seen its fair share of trouble in the last two hours. And they have come out of it all together again, in each other's arms, headed home for the holidays. The resolution of the A-story, the action-film plot, has effected a reconciliation in the marriage, fulfilling an implicit promise made in the screenplay early on. But despite our rooting interest in Holly and John as a couple, and the apparent sexual chemistry they share (the way Holly looks at John even as she keeps her distance, John's desperate search for Holly on the roof, and their exit, kissing in the limo), the marriage, we discover in the film's several sequels, doesn't last. In *Die Hard 2*, Holly is still an executive with Nakatomi. She hasn't given up her career or her life in LA. She knows who she is, what she wants and what she needs. John has tried to adapt, he's joined the LAPD (alongside Al and Dwayne). He feels emasculated by the concessions he's made to the marriage and family life. And he's itching to get back to the mean streets back east. The relationship is thrown a lifeline when at Dulles International Airport in Washington, DC, John is again called into action. He runs wild – fights terrorists and defies federal agents and airport security – and saves the day. Rescuing Holly a second time in a couple of years proves his manhood. But the very repetition made necessary by a sequel undermines the believability of the formula. How many times will Holly, a female corporate executive, really need his help? And what is the point of him – as a man – if there's nothing heroic for him to do.

In the third instalment, *Die Hard with a Vengeance* (John McTiernan, 1995), Holly is a structuring absence. John and Holly are again living on opposite coasts. They have not spoken since a fight on the telephone a year earlier. *Die Hard with a Vengeance* defers to Stuart's logline again and again. We see John struggle and narrowly escape death. Then, while safe for the moment, he contemplates calling Holly to apologise. But something always stops him: the bad guys, technology, some trouble with his newest Black sidekick (a Harlem store owner played by Samuel L. Jackson), his ego, his pride.

Jeremy Irons as Simon Peter Gruber, Hans Gruber's brother, in *Die Hard with a Vengeance* (1995)

The film ends with John's vague promise to venture west to see Lucy and maybe Holly, too, while he's at it.

*Live Free or Die Hard* (Len Wiseman, 2007), the fourth film in the franchise released nineteen years after the original, begins with the couple divorced. Holly now lives in San Francisco, the one city John regards as even more ridiculous than LA. So final is their estrangement that John's only connection to Holly is, as it is in the novel *Nothing Lasts Forever*, through their daughter, Lucy. The less said about the fifth instalment – *A Good Day to Die Hard* (John Moore), released in 2013 to mark the twenty-fifth anniversary of the original – the better, though it introduces a new McClane family member, John's estranged son, now a CIA agent. The film ends with a happy family reunion: John, John Jr and Lucy. But no Holly.

## **4** Christmas in July

*Die Hard* premiered in Los Angeles on 12 July 1988. A limited big-city release followed a few days later and a wider first run five days after that, with what they call in the business 'the platform' going ever wider as word of mouth began to spread about the film. The studio initially promoted and advertised *Die Hard* modestly, especially for an action title scheduled for the heat of the summer season, and it outperformed even the most optimistic of their expectations, breaking the $100 million mark in its first run. The *Die Hard* franchise has to date earned around $2 billion worldwide.

In 1989, *Die Hard* received four Oscar nominations: editing (Frank J. Urioste and John F. Link), sound (Don Bassman, Kevin F. Cleary, Richard Overton and Al Overton), visual effects (Richard Edlund, Al Di Sarro, Brent Boates and Thaine Morris) and sound effects editing (Stephen H. Flick and Richard Shorr). Silver and Gordon had put their money into the whammies, and the Oscar nominations rewarded the strategy. Practitioners in the respective postproduction categories recognised the work and, by extension, the studio's investment in FX talent.

After 1988, *Die Hard* became a model for the modern Hollywood action film. And its template became the stuff of industry shorthand. When the production team shopping the 1994 action film *Speed*, directed by Jan de Bont (the director of photography on *Die Hard*), pitched their film to Fox as '*Die Hard* on a bus', the executives and later most every filmgoer in America surely knew what that meant.

In 2007, anticipating the film's twenty-year anniversary, the Smithsonian National Museum of American History put on display John McClane's bloody T-shirt, in doing so commemorating the costume as an iconic artefact of 1980s

American pop culture. Ten years later, the Library of Congress selected *Die Hard* for its National Film Registry, noting the film's cultural, historical and aesthetic significance. A 2007 critics poll for the popular magazine *Entertainment Weekly* selected *Die Hard* as the number one action film of all time.[26] *Time Out*'s list of the 101 best action films assembled seventeen years later in 2024 had *Die Hard* at number one as well.[27]

After the success of *Die Hard*, Willis became a bankable movie star. Rickman too, though of a different sort. McTiernan went on to direct the brilliant Cold War action film *The Hunt for Red October* (1990); the best of the *Die Hard* sequels, *Die Hard with a Vengeance*; and an excellent remake of the stylish caper film *The Thomas Crown Affair* (1999). Then, after being implicated in an FBI sting targeting the notorious LA private eye Anthony Pellicano, McTiernan's career fell off a cliff. McTiernan had hired Pellicano in 1998 during a contentious divorce proceeding and then again in 2002 to investigate the producer Charles Roven, whom the director blamed for the failure of his *Rollerball* remake released that year. That the director was undone for lying to the FBI seems at once unlucky and ironic, and, as the director of a Reaganite cinema bliss-out, apropos.

What even the most optimistic of those who supported the production and release of *Die Hard* could never have seen coming was its ready embrace as a Christmas film. Along with *Holiday Inn* (Mark Sandrich, 1942), *Meet Me in St. Louis* (Vincente Minnelli, 1944), *It's a Wonderful Life* (Frank Capra, 1946), *Miracle on 34th Street* (George Seaton, 1947), *A Christmas Carol* (let's go with the best of a handful of adaptations: Brian Desmond Hurst, 1951), *White Christmas* (Michael Curtiz, 1954), *A Christmas Story* (Bob Clark, 1983), *Love Actually* (Richard Curtis, 2003) and *Elf* (Jon Favreau, 2003), to name just the most obvious, *Die Hard* has become for families and friends gathering at Christmas 'must see cinema', screened or streamed at the same time every year.

A debate briefly emerged online concerning the film's seasonal bona fides, but that discussion seems usefully focused on intention rather than fact – a point made abundantly clear by some very heavy hitters in film studies: David Bordwell, Kristin Thompson and Thomas Elsaesser (incidentally, the owner of the aforementioned flat in Stoke Newington where we stayed the night we didn't take Pan Am Flight 103).[28]

In a lecture later published online titled 'Die Hard and Classical/ Post-Classical Narrative', Elsaesser quipped with characteristic attitude that those on the wrong side of this debate 'cannot have watched the film carefully', as Christmas is 'embedded in both the surface and deep structure of the film'. This embedding, Elsaesser argues, is consistent with the film's evident post-classicism – its penchant for self-reference, for what now gets lumped into the broad category of 'meta', what used to be called postmodern. From the opening limo ride through the clever underscoring at the end of Die Hard, the film nods over and again to the time and the season. A quick survey follows.

During the brief ride from the airport to Nakatomi Plaza, Argyle turns on the car stereo. John predictably fails to recognise and appreciate the song that takes us into the narrative, a number made popular in the lead-in to Christmas 1987, Run-D.M.C.'s 'Christmas in Hollis'. 'Play some Christmas music,' he grouses, but only because he's not listening closely. He should at the very least recognise the song's setting – Hollis, Queens, New York – a neighbourhood he's surely passed through and maybe once upon a time policed. The song subtly plays the race card, a theme the film will take up in earnest afterwards. It also highlights Argyle's youth, and more so John's middle age. (In the novel Nothing Lasts Forever, Leland is a semi-retired consultant, an old-school former cop in late middle age.) The point here is that Argyle is from a different culture, a different generation, a different world. The song neatly sets a light and comic tone. That was always Run-D.M.C.'s calling card, which is consistent here with the tone of the tête-à-tête in the limo.

After John spies Holly's name on the directory screen, he gripes, 'Jesus,' and then absent-mindedly whistles 'Jingle Bells' to himself.

Later, as he contemplates Tony's surprisingly small shoe size, he sees a Santa hat. Willis pauses for a second and appears wistful … suggesting John taking a moment to think about his family, the ostensible reason for the trip that has taken him to the West Coast and into this current predicament. When he dispatches Tony back to Hans, the corpse is costumed with the Santa hat, and bears a message emblazoned on the sweatshirt, 'Now I have a machine gun – Ho, ho, ho.' John knows it's Christmas, and if we buy Bordwell, Thompson and Elsaesser's arguments about post-classicism, he seems to know he's in a Christmas movie. By this juncture we should too.

Later, when Al heads back to his car after checking in at Nakatomi Plaza, he sings 'Let It Snow! Let It Snow! Let It Snow!' to himself – a neat bit of foreshadowing and character development. It's fair to surmise that Al would have recognised Run-D.M.C.'s 'Christmas in Hollis', but he can't remember the lyrics to the Jule Styne/Sammy Cahn classic, made popular by singers John would more likely recognise, Frank Sinatra in 1950 and then Dean Martin sixteen years later.

As Theo nears the end of his several-stage process to crack the uncrackable safe, he touches base with Hans, who has promised an as yet undisclosed workaround for the final step: 'You better be right because it looks like this last [stage is] gonna take a miracle.' As a

former terrorist, Hans, no doubt, hates Christmas. And as an old-world product of a classical education, he finds the American – and this is Elsaesser again – 'culturally overdetermined holiday season'[29] crass and ridiculous. Tongue in cheek, Hans replies, 'It's Christmas, Theo. The time of miracles. So be of good cheer and call me when you get to the last lock.'

For those still thinking semiotics in 1988, those still noting the signs and meanings in movies: just before Hans's first in-person misadventure with John, just before he leaves his flashlight and gun on a ledge, we see some graffito, 'Merry Christmas', inked onto the partially built environment. We can only guess at its source – electricians, maybe? – but it works to remind us that one cultural difference in play here involves believing in and celebrating Christmas. Hans scoffs at the notion of Christmas miracles. And as the film's naughty not nice villain, he gets his miracle (with the 'Ode to Joy' underscoring his temporary victory) but, in his arrogance, squanders it.

As the film nears the two-hour mark, after the explosives are detonated and as John at the last-minute wriggles out from the tangled fire hose, we cut to the Tower's atrium as a Christmas tree falls into the rubble. We are inclined to wonder: will John save Christmas? The answer comes in short order, as to save Christmas,

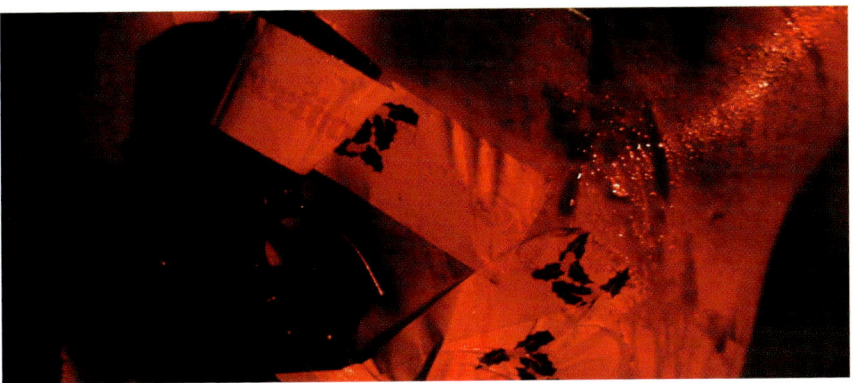

John spies some Christmas packing tape and fashions his own Christmas miracle

first Christmas must save him. John spies some Christmas packing tape, which he uses to MacGyver a gun behind his neck for the final showdown. Stretching the post-classical reading, maybe he hears what we hear, the 'Ode to Joy' softly underscoring in the sound mix.

When John emerges from the dust and smoke, Holly intones, 'Jesus.' The double entendre is intentional: Holly is remarking at his endurance. Still, it's hard to miss this seeming reference to a more famous resurrection. Holly's line prompts laughter in live screenings. But that's only because it feels a bit too on the nose.

The film ends in full Christmas mode. Amidst debris falling like the only snow LA is likely to see, Holly and John head home – well, to her home – for the holidays. Hans and Karl are dead, and for good measure Holly has just punched out Thornburg, not exactly a matter of good cheer, rather a reminder that she can take care of herself. Argyle, who had earlier commented on John's marriage without knowing much about either party, now knows a lot more. And he likes what he's seen, post-classically speaking: 'If this is your idea of Christmas, I gotta be here for New Year's.' As John and Holly kiss in the back seat, a Vaughn Monroe cover of 'Let It Snow! Let It Snow! Let It Snow!' accompanies their exit. Cut to credits. And to a Merry

Christmas, 1988 ... at least until Lockerbie, which will intervene in the meantime.

The 'Is *Die Hard* a Christmas movie?' debate was mostly made in fun. Eventually, it caught the attention of the CNN newsman Jake Tapper, prompting him to pen a short poem on the topic to the cadence of ''Twas the Night Before Christmas'.[30] Tapper posted his handiwork on Twitter, settling things, he hoped, with a simple couplet: 'That *Die Hard* is a Christmas film seems to me just a fact / I declare this without any tact.' The tweet inspired a conversation on the platform between Tapper and the *Die Hard* screenwriter, Steven E. de Souza, who here gets the last word on the subject. Asked if *Die Hard* is in fact a Christmas movie, de Souza replied: 'Yes, because the studio rejected the Purim draft.'

# Notes

**1** Andrew Britton, 'Blissing Out: The Politics of Reaganite Entertainment', *Movie* nos. 31/32 (1987).

**2** The ribbed cotton sleeveless men's T-shirt/undershirt has been associated with a certain type of man (working class, ethnic – hence the akas 'guinea-t' and 'dago-t') and a certain mode or style of masculinity (macho, uncouth, prone to violence) for decades. According to a few online forums, referring to the shirt as a 'wife-beater' dates to the 1940s and a certain Detroit man arrested for beating his wife. More relevant here are popular films featuring men costumed in ribbed-cotton sleeveless T-shirts who embody/portray this certain style of masculinity, including Marlon Brando as Stanley Kowalski in *A Streetcar Named Desire* (Elia Kazan, 1951) and James Caan as Sonny Corleone in Francis Ford Coppola's *The Godfather* twenty-one years later. That Bruce Willis as John McClane is costumed similarly is hardly inadvertent.

**3** See the graphic designer James Barnard's TikTok video. Available at: <https://www.tiktok.com/@barnardco/video/7312737509845273888> (accessed 11 November 2024). The logo transcends its branding of the building in the film to extend to the proliferation of *Die Hard* merchandise on the web. See: <https://www.etsy.com/market/nakatomi_logo> (accessed 11 November 2024). Big thanks to Martha for the inside graphic design stuff.

**4** James Chen, 'Bearer Bond: Definition, How it Works, and Why They're Valuable', *Investopedia*, 9 November 2023. Available at: <https://www.investopedia.com/terms/b/bearer_bond.asp#:~:text=Understanding%20Bearer%20Bonds,the%20bond%20value%20at%20maturity> (accessed 11 November 2024).

**5** I interviewed Jeb Stuart in 2013 for my *Essential Cinema* textbook project. An excerpt of that interview can be found in Jon Lewis, *Essential Cinema: An Introduction to Film Analysis* (Boston, MA: Cengage, 2014), p. 22. A link to the full interview is available at <http://cengagebrain.com> (accessed 11 November 2024) (alas, behind a paywall).

**6** Brian Henderson, 'Semi-Tough or Impossible: Romantic Comedy Today', *Film Quarterly* vol. 31 no. 4 (1978), pp. 11–23.

**7** Stanley Cavell, *Pursuits of Happiness* (Boston, MA: Harvard University Press, 1984).

**8** In 2022, publicists announced Willis's retirement and attributed the decision to 'aphasia', a symptom of what would later be described as frontotemporal dementia.

**9** The term 'hard body' can be traced to Susan Jeffords's book *Hard Bodies: Hollywood Masculinity in the Reagan Era* (New Brunswick, NJ: Rutgers University Press, 1993). Other books on the topic from this era include Fred Pfeil, *White Guys: Studies in Postmodern Domination and Difference* (New York: Verso, 1995), Yvonne Tasker, *Spectacular Bodies: Gender, Genre, and the Action Cinema* (London: Routledge, 1993), and Steven Cohan and Ina Rae Hark (eds), *Screening the Male: Exploring Masculinities in Hollywood Cinema* (London: Routledge, 1992).

**10** The transcript of Bly's 1998 interview with the film-maker Colleen Casto and the screenwriter Mary Dickson for their PBS/KUED series *No Safe Place* is posted at <https://www.pbs.org/kued/nosafeplace/interv/bly.html> (accessed 11 November 2024).

**11** Ibid. See also: Robert Bly, *Iron John: A Book about Men* (New York: Addison-Wesley, 1990).

**12** Fred Pfeil, 'From Pillar to Postmodern: Race, Class, and Gender in the Male Rampage Film', in Jon Lewis (ed.), *The New American Cinema* (Durham, NC: Duke University Press, 1998), pp. 146–86.

**13** Blake Snyder's website, available at: <https://savethecat.com/> (accessed 11 November 2024).

**14** The Stallone/Schwarzenegger rivalry is legendary; in the 1990s the two men could barely stand to be in the same room.

**15** Robert Venturi, Denise Scott Brown and Steven Izenour, *Learning from Las Vegas* (Boston, MA: MIT Press, 1972).

**16** Fredric Jameson, *Postmodernism, or the Cultural Logic of Late Capitalism* (Durham, NC: Duke University Press, 1992).

**17** I worked for the marketing firm Lieberman Research West, at 1900 Avenue of the Stars, a few years before the expansion of Century City and the erection of Fox Plaza. At the time, Century City struck me as downtown LA without the downtown – that is, corporate skyscrapers without the traffic going east and without the poverty that in those days so blighted downtown.

**18** The Ferrari that went out of the window was a fibreglass shell, a replica. A real, properly kept 1961 Ferrari 250 GT California, of which only fifty-six were built, would today fetch about $20 million at auction. See 'Movie Cars: Five Facts about that Ferrari in *Ferris Bueller's Day Off*'. Available at: <https://automedia.revsinstitute.org/movie-cars-five-facts-about-that-ferrari-in-ferris-buellers-day-off> (accessed 11 November 2024).

**19** John Gregory Dunne, 'Truth, Illusion, and Very Good Insurance: I'd Like to Thank the Members of the Academy', *Esquire*, July 1991, pp. 88–91.

**20** Snyder website.

**21** The timing of these whammy beats is inexact. I rounded up the times to the minute following the running-time counter as I watched the 'Five Star Collection' edition of the DVD on the VLC player on my computer. Timecodes across versions and formats vary. The timecodes noted here nonetheless accurately characterise the relative duration and location within the film of its essential beats.

**22** Louis Althusser, 'Ideology and Ideological State Apparatuses', in *Lenin and Philosophy and Other Essays*, trans. Ben Brewster (New York: Monthly Review Press, 1971), pp. 121–76.

**23** On Valentine's Day 2024 some stupid idiots took their guns to a Super Bowl celebration in Kansas City, got into a stupid dispute and stupidly tried to settle that dispute by shooting at each other, oblivious to thousands of innocent bystanders, several of whom were shot (one dead, at least twenty-two seriously injured) in the fracas. It would have been just another day in the

USA for me if not for a text I received that morning from my son Adam, who was working with the mayor's office there. When he sent the text he was sequestered underneath the Kansas City Union Station, along with many other city workers and bystanders moved by police out of the line of fire. For the record: I hate guns. And I lament the current attitude among American lawmakers that gun control can't be implemented even when most Americans want it.

**24** Available at: <https://www.reddit.com/r/movies/comments/khxzap/why_the_confusion_with_shoot_the_glass/> (accessed 11 November 2024). Special thanks to Sebastian Heiduschke, who teaches German here at Oregon State University, for the nuanced translations.

**25** 'Happy Trails' was the theme song sung by Rogers and his wife Dale Evans on their radio and TV shows.

**26** Marc Bernardin, 'The Big Bang', *Entertainment Weekly*, 22 June 2007, pp. 24–30.

**27** Joshua Rothkopf, 'The Best Action Movies of All Time', *Time Out*, 25 January 2024. Available at: <https://www.timeout.com/film/the-101-best-action-movies-ever-made> (accessed 11 November 2024).

**28** Thomas Elsaesser, '*Die Hard* and Classical/Post-Classical Narrative', *Mind the Screen: Thomas Elseasser on Cinema, Art, and Media*, 14 January 2017. Available at: <https://mindthescreen.wordpress.com/2017/01/14/classicalpost-classical-narrative-die-hard/> (accessed 11 November 2024); and Kristin Thompson and David Bordwell, 'Not just a Christmas Movie: *Die Hard* on the Big Screen', *Observations on Film Art*, 17 December 2019. Available at: <https://www.davidbordwell.net/blog/2019/12/17/not-just-a-christmas-movie-die-hard-on-the-big-screen/> (accessed 11 November 2024).

**29** Elsaesser, '*Die Hard* and Classical/Post-Classical Narrative'.

**30** The poem was originally titled 'A Visit from St Nicholas' and published anonymously in the *Troy, New York Sentinel* on 23 December 1823. It was later attributed to Clement Clarke Moore and is now better known by its akas: 'The Night Before Christmas' and ''Twas the Night Before Christmas'.

**Image credits**

Images from *A Streetcar Named Desire* (Elia Kazan, 1951), © Charles K. Feldman Group Productions; *Moonlighting* (Glenn Gordon Caron, 1985–9), ABC Circle Films/Picturemaker Productions; *Lethal Weapon* (Richard Donner, 1987), Warner Bros./Silver Pictures; *Terminator 2: Judgment Day* (James Cameron, 1991), © Carolco Pictures, Inc.; *Predator* (John McTiernan, 1987), Amercent Films/American Independent Partners/Twentieth Century Fox Film Corporation; *Die Hard with a Vengeance* (John McTiernan, 1995), © Cinergi Pictures Entertainment/Cinergi Productions N.V., Inc./Twentieth Century Fox Film Corporation.

# Credits

**Die Hard**
USA
1988

**Directed by**
John McTiernan
**Production Company**
The Gordon Company
Silver Pictures

Twentieth Century Fox
presents
A Gordon Company/
Silver Pictures production
A John McTiernan film

© 1988 Twentieth
Century Fox Film
Corporation

**Executive Producer**
Charles Gordon
**Produced by**
Lawrence Gordon
Joel Silver
**Associate Producer/
Unit Production
Manager**
Beau E. L. Marks
**Production Executive**
Riley Kathryn Ellis
**Production Associate**
Tamara Smith
**Production
Co-ordinators**
Lynne Taylor
Elizabeth Galloway
**Production Accountant**
K. Lenna Kunkel

**Assistant Production
Accountants**
Alison Harstedt
Jyllel Syage
**Location Managers**
Joel B. Marx
Ken H. Rosen
**Assistant Location
Manager**
Antoinette Simmrin
**Location Liaison**
Dan Carroll
**Production Assistants**
Brook Altman
Kari Ann Messina
Lisa Miller
Frank Reinhard
Phil Robinson
**Assistants to
Lawrence Gordon**
Kellett Tighe
Shari Schneider
**Assistants to
Joel Silver**
Susan Joy Beallor
Ladd Rosenberg-Vance
**Assistants to
John McTiernan**
Carol Land
Pamela Alessandrelli
**Assistant to
Charles Gordon**
Annie Saunders
**Assistants to
Bruce Willis**
Deborah Johnson
Clare Leavenworth
**2nd Unit Director**
Beau E. L. Marks

**1st Assistant Director**
Benjamin Rosenberg
**2nd Assistant Director**
Terry Miller Jr
**2nd 2nd Assistant
Director**
Michael Alan Kahn
**DGA Trainee**
Paula Foster
**Script Supervisor**
Marion Tumen
**Casting**
Jackie Burch
**Casting (Associate)**
Ferne Cassel
**Casting (Extras)**
Central Casting
Carl Joy
**Screenplay by**
Jeb Stuart
Steven E. de Souza
**Based on the Novel by**
Roderick Thorp
**Director of Photography**
Jan de Bont
**Camera Operators**
Michael Ferris
Michael Scott
M. Todd Henry
**Camera Assistants**
Brian Armstrong
John Ellingwood
Les Zell
**Gaffer**
Ed Ayer
**Musco Light Operators**
Roger Spurgeon
Ron Kunecke
Mike DeMeyer
Brad Chelesvig

**[Gaffer's] Best Boys**
Michael Franz
Blaise Dahlquist
**Electricians**
Brink Brydon
Steven C. Hodge
Doug Yonker
**Key Grip**
William E. Decker III
**Best Boy Grips**
Bernie Schwartz
John Donnelly
**Dolly Grip**
Glenn 'Bear' Davis
**Grips**
Brian Joe Holechek
Matthew Nelson
Jim Rankin
**Still Photographer**
Peter Sorel
Bob Isenberg
**Visual Effects
Produced by**
Richard Edlund
**Special Visual Effects
in 65mm**
Boss Film Corporation
**Director of Photography
(Boss)**
William Neil
**Visual Effects
Art Director (Boss)**
Brent Boates
**Visual Effects Editor
(Boss)**
Dennis Michelson
**Chief Financial Officer
(Boss)**
Donald R. Fly

**Special Effects Foreman
(Boss)**
Thaine Morris
**Optical Department
Supervisor (Boss)**
Chris Regan
**Model Shop Supervisor
(Boss)**
Mark Stetson
**Special Projects
Supervisor (Boss)**
Garry Waller
**Chief Engineer (Boss)**
Gene Whiteman
**Chief Matte Artist (Boss)**
Matthew Yuricich
**Assistant to Richard
Edlund (Boss)**
Claire Wilson
**Production Co-ordinator
(Boss)**
Michael Van Himbergen
**Optical Supervisor
'Die Hard' (Boss)**
Al Cox
**Optical Camera
Operator (Boss)**
James Sleeper
**Optical Line-up (Boss)**
Kevin Clark
Peter Yanovitch
**Negative Developer
(Boss)**
Paul Jenson
**Camera Operator (Boss)**
Clinton Palmer
**1st Assistant
Cameraman (Boss)**
Stefanie Wiseman

**Still Photographer
(Boss)**
Virgil Mirano
**Technical Animation
Supervisor (Boss)**
Samuel Recinos
**Technical Production
Assistants (Boss)**
Maura Alvarez
Meg Freeman
Lisa Krepela
**Assistant Visual Effects
Editor (Boss)**
Debra Wolff
**Effects Technician
(Boss)**
Daniel Hutten
**Chief Lighting Tech
(Boss)**
Robert Eyslee
**Key Grip (Boss)**
Patrick Van Auken
**Stage Assistants (Boss)**
Kelly Kerby
Chrissa Owens
Jeff Rand
**Chief Model Maker
(Boss)**
Patrick McClung
**Model Construction
Foreman (Boss)**
Milius Romyn
**Model Makers (Boss)**
Jarek Alfer
Kent Gebo
Bruce MacRae
Suzy Schneider
Dennis Schultz
Dana Yuricich

**Stand-by Model Maker (Boss)**
Alan Faucher

**Model Electronics (Boss)**
Richard Chronister

**Model Effects Key Man (Boss)**
Robert Johnston

**Model Effects (Boss)**
Paul Sabourin

**Model Painter (Boss)**
Ron Gress

**Model Helicopter Consultant (Boss)**
Larry Jolly

**Chief Miniature Moldmaker (Boss)**
David Schwartz

**Design Engineer (Boss)**
Mark West

**Chief Electronics Engineer (Boss)**
Philip Crescenzo

**Precision Cinetechnician (Boss)**
Ken Dudderar

**Production Accountant (Boss)**
Maryjane Zelicskovics

**Special Effects Co-ordinator**
Al Di Sarro

**Special Effects Foreman**
William Aldridge

**Special Effects Assistants**
James Camomile
Bruno Van Zeebroeck
Andrew Sebok
Jay Bartus
Richard L. Thompson
Dennis Dion
Larry Deunger
Darrell Prichett
Joe Ramsey
Jay Hirsch
Steve Suits
Richard Zarro
Hal Bigger
Michael A. Tice

**Special Effects Transportation**
Patrick R. Gordon

**Video and Graphic Displays by**
Video Image
Rhonda C. Gunner
Richard E. Hollander
Gregory L. McMurry
John C. Wash

**Film Editors**
Frank J. Urioste
John F. Link

**Assistant Editors**
Derek G. Brechin
Gregory M. Gerlich
Bryan Carroll

**2nd Assistant Editors**
Edward Malone
Jeff Gullo

**Production Designer**
Jackson DeGovia

**Art Director**
John R. Jensen

**Assistant Art Directors**
William J. Durrell Jr
Craig Edgar

**Set Designers**
E. C. Chen
Roland Hill

**Set Decorator**
Phil M. Leonard

**Set Dressers**
Richard Boris
Mike Bruner
Gus Feederle
Efrain Gonzalez
Kirk B. Jones
Donald Kaeding
Steve Nelson

**Lead Man**
Bill Fannon Jr

**Illustrator**
John L. Jensen

**Property Master**
Tommy 'Tom' Tomlinson

**Assistant Property Master**
Michael Blaze

**Construction Co-ordinator**
Bruce J. Gfeller

**Construction Foreman**
Steve Callas

**Construction Paint Foreman**
Dick Girod

**Production Painter**
Jimmy Jay Hinkle

**Costume Designer**
Marilyn Vance-Straker

**Costume Supervisor**
Barry Delaney

**Women's Set Costumer**
Barbara Siebert Bolticoff

**Men's Set Costumer**
Michael J. Voght

**Additional Costumer**
Victoria Snow
**Costumer to**
**Bruce Willis**
Charles Mercuri
**Make-up Supervisor**
Scott H. Eddo
**Make-up Artists**
Wes Dawn
Jim Kail
**Hair Stylist**
Paul Abascal
**Hair Stylist to**
**Bruce Willis**
Josée Normand
**Additional Optical**
**Effects and Title Design**
R/Greenberg Assoc., Inc.
**Colour Timers**
Bob Hagans
Dale Grahn
**Music by**
Michael Kamen
**Orchestra Conducted by**
Michael Kamen
**Additional**
**Orchestrations by**
Bruce Babcock
Chris Boardman
Philip Giffin
Fi Trench
**Music Producer**
Stephen E. McLaughlin
**Music Editing**
Segue Music
**Supervising Music**
**Editor**
Christopher Brooks
**Scoring Mixer**
Armin Steiner

**Scoring Engineers**
Walt Borchers
Terry Brown
Chuck Garsha
**Sound Mixer**
Al Overton
**Recordists**
Robert Renga
Craig Heath
**Machine Operator**
Phyllis Drury
**Maintenance Engineer**
Ken Stone
**Boom Operator**
Dennis Jones
**Cable Operator**
Todd Overton
**Dubbing Projectionist**
Alex Algarin
**Re-recording Mixers**
Don Bassman
Kevin F. Cleary
Richard Overton
**Supervising Dialogue**
**Editor**
George Anderson
**Dialogue Editors**
Jeff Rosen
Cindy Marty
**Assistant Sound Editors**
Destiny Borden
Oscar Mitt
**Post-production**
**Dialogue**
Norman B. Schwartz
**Negative Cutter**
Gary Burritt
**Assistant Dialogue**
**Editor**
Kevin Barlia

**Sound Effects by**
Stephen H. Flick
Richard Shorr
**Sound Effects Editors**
David Stone
Catherine Shorr
**ADR Recordist**
Dennis Rogers
**ADR Mixer**
Kevin Carpenter
**Supervising ADR Editor**
Hank Salerno
**ADR Editors**
James R. Simcik
Ronald Sinclair
Bill Voigtlander
**ADR (Assistant Editors)**
Rosemarie Wheeler
Sherrie Bayer Burke
**ADR (Apprentice**
**Editors)**
Lisa M. Risen
Matthew Peerce
**Foley Mixer**
Lee Tinkham
**Foley Editors**
Ron Bartlett
Rick Mitchell
**Foley by**
Vanessa Ament
Robin Harlan
**Stunt Co-ordinator**
Charles Picerni
**Stunts by**
Ken Bates
Janet Brady
Nick Brett
Jophery Brown
Kurt Bryant
Brian Christensen

Gil Combs
Kerrie Cullen
Kenny Endoso
Andrew Epper
Randy Hall
Norman Howell
Keii Johnston
Henry M. Kingi
Julius Le Flore
Fred Lerner
Michael Marasco
Don McGovern
John Meier
Alan Oliney
Victor Paul
Charles Picerni Jr
Paul V. Picerni Jr
Steve Picerni
Bernie Pock
Chad Randall
R. A. Rondell
Benjamin Rosenberg
John Sherrod
Russell Solberg
Steve Vandeman
George Wilbur
Glenn Wilder
Dick Ziker

**Police Technical
Adviser**
Art Fransen

**Military Technical
Adviser**
L. Gary Goldman

**Dolby Stereo Consultant**
David W. Gray

**Trainer to Bruce Willis**
Keith Cubba

**Picture Car Co-ordinator**
Stanley Webber

**Transportation
Co-ordinator**
Myra L. Hill

**Transportation
Captains**
Dean Mason
Jim Nordberg

**Caterer**
Tony Kerum

**Craft Service**
Rick Chavez

**First Aid**
Marilynn B. Frank

**Weapons Specialist**
Michael Papac

**Special Weapons
Training**
Bobby Bass

**Pilots**
Peter McKernan
Peter McKernan Jr
Alan Purwin
Charles A. Tamburro
Michael Tamburro
Tony Tamburro

**Publicity Co-ordinator**
Andrew Lipschultz

**Knives Provided by**
Jack W. Crain,
Weatherford, Texas

**Special Ceramic Vessels
Provided by**
Paul Chaleff and Tod M.
Volpe, LA and NY

**Songs**
'Singin' in the Rain', by
Arthur Freed and Nacio
Herb Brown; 'Winter
Wonderland', by Felix
Bernard and Dick Smith;
'Christmas in Hollis', by
Joseph Simmons, Darryl
McDaniels and Jason
Mizell, performed by Run-
D.M.C., courtesy of Profile
Records, Inc.; 'Skeletons',
written and performed by
Stevie Wonder, courtesy
of Motown Record Corp.;
'Let It Snow! Let It Snow!
Let It Snow', by Sammy
Cahn and Jule Styne,
performed by Vaughn
Monroe, courtesy of MCA
Records

**Special Thanks to**
C. Itoh Electronics, Inc.;
Carver Corporation;
Control Data Corp. &
ETA Systems, Inc.; Eldon
Office Products; Hamilton
Sorter Company, Inc.;
Javelin Electronics;
Pitney Bowes, Inc.; Ford
Showcase; Freightliner;
Hadler Public Relations;
Norm Marshall &
Associates, Inc.; Unique
Product Placement; Vista
Group; Allen Pena, KKTV,
Los Angeles; Dick Beving
and George Meehan, City
of Los Angeles Motion
Picture Coordination
Office; Eli Tawil, West
Los Angeles Area, LA
Police Department;
Jim Gembala and the
residents of Century Hill

Condominiums; Maria Morris and the residents of Century Park Place Condiminiums; Georgian Francisco and the staff of The Century Plaza Hotel and Tower; Patty Brewer and the management of The Century Plaza Towers; JMB Property Management; Marriott Corporation

**CAST**
**Bruce Willis**
John McClane
**Bonnie Bedelia**
Holly Gennaro McClane
**Reginald VelJohnson**
Sergeant Al Powell
**Paul Gleason**
Dwayne T. Robinson
**De'Voreaux White**
Argyle
**William Atherton**
Richard Thornburg
**Hart Bochner**
Harry Ellis
**James Shigeta**
Joe Takagi
**Alan Rickman**
Hans Gruber, terrorist
**Alexander Godunov**
Karl, terrorist
**Bruno Doyon**
Franco, terrorist
**Andreas Wisniewski**
Tony, terrorist
**Clarence Gilyard Jr**
Theo, terrorist

**Joey Plewa**
Alexander, terrorist
**Lorenzo Caccialanza**
Marco, terrorist
**Gerard Bonn**
Kristoff, terrorist
**Dennis Hayden**
Eddie, terrorist
**Al Leong**
Uli, terrorist
**Gary Roberts**
Heinrich, terrorist
**Hans Buhringer**
Fritz, terrorist
**Wilhelm von Homburg**
James, terrorist
**Robert Davi**
Big Johnson, FBI agent
**Grand L. Bush**
Little Johnson, FBI agent
**Bill Marcus**
Walt, city engineer
**Rick Ducommun**
city worker
**Matt Landers**
Captain Mitchell
**Carmine Zozzora**
Rivers
**Dustyn Taylor**
Ginny
**George Christy**
Hasseldorf
**Anthony Peck**
young cop
**Cheryl Baker**
**Richard Parker**
man & woman
**David Ursin**
Harvey Johnson

**Mary Ellen Trainor**
Gail Wallens
**Diana James**
supervisor
**Shelley Pogoda**
dispatcher
**Selma Archerd**
**Scot Bennett**
**Rebecca Broussard**
**Kate Finlayson**
**Shanna Higgins**
**Kym Malin**
hostages
**Taylor Fry**
Lucy McClane
**Noah Land**
John Jr
**Betty Carvalho**
Paulina
**Kip Waldo**
convenience store clerk
**Mark Goldstein**
station manager
**Tracy Reiner**
Thornburg's assistant
**Rick Cicetti**
**Fred Lerner**
guards
**Bill Margolin**
producer
**Bob Jennings**
**Bruce P. Schultz**
cameramen
**David Katz**
soundman
**Robert Lesser**
businessman
**Stella Hall**
stewardess

**Terri Lynn Doss**
girl at airport
**Jon E. Greene**
boy at airport
**P. Randall Bowers**
kissing man
**Michele Laybourn**
girl in window

**Production Details**
35mm (printed film)
2.39:1
Colour (DeLuxe)
Dolby Stereo
MPAA no.: 29160
Running time:
132 minutes

**Release Details**
US theatrical release
on 20 July 1988 by
Twentieth Century Fox
UK theatrical release
on 3 February 1989 by
Twentieth Century Fox
Film Company